D1459665

The Blended Family

Tom and Adrienne Frydenger

Chosen Books

A Division of Baker Book House
Grand Rapids, Michigan 49516

Library of Congress Cataloging in Publication Data

Frydenger, Tom.
    The blended family.

1. Family—Religious life.   2. Remarriage—Religious aspects—
Christianity.   I. Frydenger, Adrienne.   II. Title.
BV4526.2.F79   1985   248.4   84-20068
ISBN 0-8007-9094-4

A Chosen Book
Copyright © 1984 by Tom and Adrienne Frydenger
Chosen Books are published by Fleming H. Revell
a divison of Baker Book House Company
P.O. Box 6287, Grand Rapids, MI 49516-6287

ISBN: 0-8007-9094-4

Eighth printing, August 1995

Printed in the United States of America

The Blended Family

To our fathers,

Donald J. Brinkman and William O. Frydenger

*They didn't live to see our dreams come true,
but they always believed in them.*

Acknowledgments

Special thanks:

To Steve Hamon, counselor/therapist, for critiquing our perspective on blended families.

To Jim Klein, counselor/therapist, for assisting us in our review of related literature.

To Jessica Stricklin, attorney, for her comments on legal issues concerning blended families.

To Grandma Frydenger and Grandma Brinkman for the many hours of babysitting that allowed us to write in peace (and quiet).

And to all of the stepparents who participated in our blended family group sessions or allowed us into their lives with the hope that their experiences would be of benefit to others.

Contents

1

Looking Back Down the Aisle

I straightened my tie for the hundredth time and looked through the slightly opened doorway of the sanctuary. It seemed every seat was taken, but my groomsmen were still ushering guests down the long aisle. I closed the door and fingered my tie nervously.

"Larry, you're sure you have the ring."

"I'm sure."

"You're positive?"

"Relax, Tom. After all, today is only going to change your whole life."

Only going to change my whole life. I'd lived through so many changes already my cocoon was getting thin. And here I was, about to be transformed from Tom Frydenger: single person, into Tom Frydenger: bona fide husband and father. And *father!* Soon two little girls would walk down the aisle and into my life. What a responsibility!

Just a few months before, I had envisioned myself traveling widely, employing my profession of family counseling wherever needs arose. And not so much wanting to travel alone, I discovered that two tensions tugged at my dream:

wanting a wife, and being panic-stricken I'd find one. To help reduce some of the terror of being accountable to someone other than myself for a lifetime, I decided to devise a "Perfect Wife List." If I could find someone who actually fit my list, I'd have the perfect marriage. Although the list was elaborate, it certainly didn't include a woman who already had children.

Then along came Adrienne. It was a cold, snowy January morning when she walked through my office door and brought wonderful chaos into my life.

I had seen Adrienne several times at church and had managed to have myself introduced to her. It was a very short introduction—"Hello. Nice to meet you, too. Good-bye." Then she was on her way out the door.

But that was O.K., I reasoned. I wasn't planning on marrying her, I just wanted to date her. Besides she had two children, a circumstance which automatically triggered my "Slow—Children" caution sign.

Adrienne had come to the office to work on a children's corner for the waiting room, but stopped to talk with the secretary. I overheard her mention she would like to speak to the head of our psychological practice concerning a personal matter and—always ready to be the knight in shining armor—I jumped into action. In a moment I was in the waiting room, telling her my associate was out, and asking if I could be of service. She surprised me by answering yes.

Time flew as we talked in my office and went out to lunch together. When finally we parted, I knew the rest of the afternoon was shot. I couldn't concentrate on anything. All I could think of was Adrienne and the list. Just thinking about the commitment of marriage was enough to make noncommittal me break out in a cold sweat, and here I was starting to fall for a woman with two children from a previous marriage.

As time went on, Adrienne and I had long conversations on the telephone about our interests, our faith and our ideas on marriage. Through these conversations I learned that she was struggling with ambivalent feelings concerning remarriage. She told me that she would read a particular Bible verse over and over: "For your Maker is your husband—the Lord Almighty is his name . . ." (Isaiah 54:5a). Some days she found it very comforting to know the Lord would protect and keep her while she was without a flesh-and-blood husband. On those days she would think about how well she and the girls were adjusting to a single-parent household.

But on other days, she wanted to marry again. She wanted someone to share special traditions, to fill the void left in the family and to help with the responsibility of running the household. She especially wanted her children to have a loving, guiding father image at home. Yet, she wasn't sure she was up to the work involved in establishing new, intimate family relationships.

As our interest in each other grew, we decided it was time I became acquainted with her children. I had no qualms about meeting Jennifer. I was convinced that she, like most two-year-olds, would cuddle right up to me. Nichole, being older, was a different story. I expected resentment and resistance to my presence in her mother's life. As it worked out, my first meeting was with Nichole.

Trying to be one step ahead of an eight-year-old was not all child's play. I role-played our meeting conversation several times in my mind, and rehearsed various approaches, and responses to what I anticipated Nichole's behavior would be. If she did this, I would do that. If she did that, I would do this.

Adrienne introduced me to Nichole one Sunday morning before worship service. As the three of us sat together, I could feel Nichole sizing me up. I became so involved in the sermon I barely noticed her inching toward me. And before I had time to analyze the situation, she had cuddled up under my arm and sleepily lain her head on my chest.

I was amazed. It was so easy. With the afterglow of success hovering over me, I couldn't wait to meet Jennifer after church.

I was so certain Jennifer would accept me at first sight I confidently told her mother, "All babies and little children love me." My confidence was quickly shaken, however, when Adrienne returned from the nursery with Jennifer and brought her to the church kitchen where Nichole and I were waiting. Before I had an opportunity to wiggle her toes or tickle her cheek, Jennifer opened her mouth and shrieked. Wanting absolutely nothing to do with me, she sobbed and screamed until I left the room.

Completely flustered, and wondering where I went wrong, I knew I had to try again. When the cries had subsided I slowly walked back into the room. Within seconds Jennifer spotted me, puckered up and began crying anew, picking up more volume with each shriek. As I left the room for the second time I felt my successful afterglow going up in smoke. Needless to say, it took a little more time for me to win Jennifer's acceptance.

The rustle of the crowd rising to its feet drew my attention to the back of the church. Somehow, on shaky legs, I had managed to follow my best man through the side door and up to the altar rail. Jennifer and Nichole had already walked down the aisle as the organist played the wedding march. In spite of my nervousness, when I saw Adrienne and her father round the turn and start toward us, I couldn't help grinning like the Cheshire cat.

As we held hands and said our vows to one another, I was acutely aware of the presence of Jennifer and Nichole. I knew, figuratively speaking, I was holding more than one hand. For in that moment, we became what is termed a blended family.

In the years since the wedding, we have discovered that forming a new family system isn't easy. Becoming a blended family means mixing, mingling, scrambling and sometimes muddling our way through delicate family issues, complicated relationships, and individual differences, hurts and fears. But through it all we are learning to love like a family.

2

Laying the Foundation

Brothers, I do not consider myself yet to have taken hold of it. But one thing I do: Forgetting what is behind and straining toward what is ahead, I press on toward the goal to win the prize for which God has called me heavenward in Christ Jesus.

(Philippians 3:13-14)

Paul advised his friends at Philippi to let go of those things in the past that would keep them from making daily progress. His advice is relevant to today's blended family. A new family system needs to build on a strong foundation, and *can*, once the crumbles of the past are cleared away. I have found through counseling in my private practice and through personal experience that the most common negative influences affecting blended family relationships are feelings of guilt and failure, and grief over loss.

Adrienne and I had been married a little over a year when these influences on our marriage left me feeling certain I was failing her as a husband. She became quiet and distant, and I didn't know why. One evening, for instance, she called the girls and me in for dinner. We all sat down, I prayed for the meal, and Adrienne burst into tears.

"No one in this family ever comes to the table the first time I call. Look at this dinner—the corn is cold, the mashed potatoes are cold and . . . and the meatballs look like they were cooked in a grease glaze."

Adrienne sobbed into her napkin while the girls and I exchanged bewildered glances.

The next night when dinner was announced, the three of us nearly fell over each other to make it to the table on the first call. There we sat, each smiling at our own promptness when Adrienne said, "The spaghetti's all glumped together and I burnt the garlic bread."

Our attempts at humor failed ("You made a new dish, Mommy, Spaghetti Glump!") as Adrienne ate her meal in silence aside from small sniffles.

This continued for several weeks. Since I couldn't get any explanations from her at home, I decided to take her out. We went to a nice quiet restaurant, and as soon as we had settled into a booth, I got right down to business.

"Adrienne, I can't take this any longer. What is it? What am I doing wrong?"

"I'm not sure I want to tell you," she finally managed to say.

"Hey," I responded, smiling, "I'm a counselor. I've heard everything. I can handle it. I'm tough."

"Well," she said quietly after taking my hand, "I miss my first marriage."

I was crushed.

As I cleared my throat to speak, my words faded into thought: *I'm not that tough!*

Adrienne responded instantly to my crestfallen look and

began pouring out what she was feeling. She told me how much she longed for her children to have only one father and one mother, one house with one set of family traditions. And she felt like a failure for allowing such an upheaval in their lives.

Once Adrienne had explained to me her feelings of loss, several things took place. She stopped feeling guilty over what was a normal reaction and realized that missing her nuclear family dream did not mean she was being disloyal to me. She also found the person in the best position to help her was the very person she had been keeping things from all along: me! And when I realized that Adrienne's actions were based on the grief she was experiencing, I was able to stop wasting time on my own introspection about what I was doing wrong and begin to help her.

We talked for hours about her feelings of grief over loss and what could have been.

She reflected, "I know those mistakes are forgiven, but I still agonize over the possible consequences my children might have to pay for the rest of their lives."

No one sincerely enters marriage expecting it to end in divorce. Most people, like Adrienne, have a "happy-ever-after" image of marriage: a nuclear family with one dad, one mom and one set of children.

Divorce not only brings the loss of that family dream, but the loss of the relationships within it. Regardless of who wanted the divorce, there is a relationship loss with the ex-mate. The non-custodial parent experiences the loss of a daily parent-child relationship with the children. Along with these losses comes the loss of extended family relationships.

The feelings of loss are greatly magnified around Thanksgiving, Christmas, vacation time or other family-oriented days. This may explain the seemingly unexplainable feelings of depression experienced by both parents and children at those times. Adrienne spent the weekend in tears when the girls first went to their grandmother's with their dad for Thanksgiving. She knew she would never again be a part of that family's special traditions.

Adrienne's feelings of loss were compounded by the feelings of guilt and failure from not making a successful go of her first marriage. That night in the restaurant she told me how she kept going over and over every mistake she could think of in her first marriage. On top of that, someone whose judgment she greatly respected told her that God's best plan for her life was that she still be in her first marriage, and that anything outside of that was second-rate.

Adrienne's guilt grew as she began wondering if her second marriage was only second-rate in God's eyes. "I'm not operating each day in faith," she explained, "but in condemnation. If I failed in my first marriage when the Lord was with me, what chance do I have in my second marriage? And I felt I couldn't talk this over with you, Tom," she added. "I was afraid you would misunderstand your 'second-class' rating."

Her sense of failure affected the whole family. She tried to hide her "imperfections"—as well as Nichole's and Jennifer's—from me. If the children misbehaved when I wasn't around, she kept it to herself. Their misbehavior only seemed to magnify her sense of failure. "I've actually been keeping the girls at a distance from you because of my own insecurity. What if this marriage failed? How would that affect my children? I have unconsciously been trying to protect them from possible hurt if I failed again."

Then she told me of a dream she had had that seemed to reveal her true motivations. In her dream she and I were walking together in our backyard in bright summer sunlight. As we walked and talked, she glanced over to her left and was startled to see a tall, glistening white wall with healthy green plants at the base. The sunlight on the wall made it so brilliantly white it was breathtaking. But as she looked closer at the porcelain-like finish, she noticed horrible, slimy slugs worming their way up the center of the wall, leaving their sticky tracks behind. Instead of pointing the unusual sight out to me, she quickly steered me away from the wall and out of the backyard.

It took some time for the strange dream to sink in, but when it did, she realized her wall was "whitewashed" for me. The slugs were all the mistakes she thought too ugly for me to see.

When Adrienne expressed her feelings, it not only helped her find relief from pressures she had been carrying, it helped me stop questioning my adequacy as her husband. I knew that if she trusted me enough to tell me what she was going through, she really loved me and felt good about our relationship.

Mates are in an ideal situation to be supportive if they can put their spouse's feelings ahead of their own. Even though I wanted to, I couldn't erase Adrienne's feelings of loss, failure or insecurity, but I could be loving and supportive. And I could encourage her to count on God's love, guidance and healing touch in our blended family.

Different couples contend with different problems in their marriages, but some issues that cause conflict between mates are more prevalent than others.

In a study on marriage and divorce, individuals who had just gone through a divorce in their first marriage were asked to rank in order what they considered the major causes of their divorces. Partner's immaturity was ranked highest, with sexual difficulties, lack of marriage readiness, in-law interference, values, social adjustment, child-rearing and finances following in that order.

Child-rearing, the seventh listed cause of divorce in first marriages, was the *main* cause for divorce in second marriages. (Following were: finances, relatives, value systems and sharing of tasks.)

That being the case, a solid foundation must include a realistic look at how remarriage affects children, and how children affect remarriage.

Dating: It Takes Time

The first of four foundation stones is simply this: Take all the time you need to get to know your future mate and his or her children.

Rearing stepchildren is not easy and the issues related to their care often produce more stress than many couples can handle. This is why it is imperative to take the children into consideration from the very beginning of the dating relationship. The "new" parent-to-be is not just developing a relationship with one person; he (or she, as the case may be) is becoming involved in a whole family system.

This was clearly exhibited by a young woman named Susan who came to me for counseling. Susan had fought the divorce initiated by her husband, but it went through. Convinced that their difficulties arose because she was a Christian and her first husband wasn't, she married Stan, a Christian, within two months of her divorce. Susan expected Stan, who had never been married before and knew little about children, to add the missing element of her first marriage and fill the role of the perfect Christian husband and father.

Just a few weeks into their marriage, Susan had a big

disagreement with Stan over a discipline problem. Her youngest child, Joey, had been a pain in the neck all day long. He had antagonized Susan, his brother and sister, the children in the neighborhood and any other form of plant or animal life he could find. By late afternoon he had the whole household in an uproar.

The moment Stan walked in the door was the very moment Craig, the eldest child, decided to end Joey's reign of terror. Screaming angrily, Craig landed a solid punch on Joey's shoulder and sent him flying across the room and into Stan.

Stan, only seeing Craig's aggression, paddled him and went to Joey's aid. Craig ran out of the room yelling, "It's not fair!", Joey rolled on the floor, shrieking in mock pain, and Cassie, the middle child, ran over to Stan and screamed, "Why did you spank my brother? You're not our dad! You can't do that!"

Susan, amidst all the turmoil, picked up Joey, pulled Cassie off Stan, and ran after a sobbing Craig. Stan was left standing in the living room, confused, crushed and feeling like an invader in a family system he knew nothing about.

The problem actually started way back with Susan's motivation for remarriage. She moved impulsively, fearful of being alone and solely responsible for her children. Wanting to fill the void left by divorce is understandable, but filling it with the first person who seems willing can be disastrous. Marrying for reasons of loneliness, insecurity or for the sake of the children is making a big mistake.

Susan's and Stan's problems were further complicated by not dating long enough to understand each person in the future family. If Stan had spent more time observing and interacting with Susan's children, he would have been better equipped to judge the chaos in progress upon walking in the front door. Being aware of Craig's tendency to hold things in until they reached the explosive level, Stan might have immediately wondered who or what had served as his detonator. Having been around Joey when he was in one of his super-pest moods would have cast a suspicious light in his direction.

With that background, Stan might have walked in, sat both boys in chairs, extracted the day's events and gotten the correct information. Not only would that have given the boys a chance to cool off, but it would have involved Susan in the discipline process. Together they could have decided on consequences for both boys, leaving Cassie without any reason to play the protector.

If Susan and Stan had viewed dating as an integral part of preparing for marriage, there would have been less trauma in the early months of their lives together.

A good principle, when planning remarriage, is to date your future mate long enough for everyone, including your children, to act naturally around each other. The children may behave perfectly while in church, but home is a different arena. The same can be true of adults. It is easy to turn on the charm or patience for a few hours at a time when you know you can always go home and recuperate, but sooner or later the armor has to come off and reveal the real you.

While Adrienne and I were dating, I agreed to take Nichole to the Six Flags amusement park. Up until then Adrienne saw me as the super father image, able to handle the children's problems with ease. Nichole was still in the "Isn't he swell?" and "Wouldn't he make a neat father?" frame of mind. And I was, in spite of my clinical knowledge and experience, under the misconception that Adrienne's children were beyond bad behavior. Taking an eight-year-old girl to an amusement park may not sound like the greatest challenge in the world, but to a single man about to be a father it was about all the challenge I needed.

Part of my mistake in choosing an amusement park as a "trial family outing," was the fact that I was born with a handicap and walk with an uneven gait. Adrienne and the girls loved and accepted me in spite of it, but they had yet to experience my limitations because of it. Since it affected my sense of balance, carnival rides reeked havoc with it. When I was young and reckless I would tackle all the rides no matter how dizzy and sick I became. But as an adult wanting to impress two ladies on a family outing, it would seem inappropriate to turn green and sprawl out on a bench, fighting to keep down my lunch.

The day started out shaky. We got a late start that put us hours behind schedule. Halfway to St. Louis, it started raining. It rained and I drove. It rained more and I got lost. The longer I drove around in the rain the quieter Nichole became. Finally, she leaned forward and asked, "Are we lost?"

Not wanting to break the bad news to her all at once, I answered, "Well, I know we're somewhere near St. Louis."

"Terrific," she answered and sank back into her seat, sulking.

She sulked, I drove and it poured.

Finally, to my immense relief—and as the rain began tapering off—Adrienne suggested we turn around and go back home. Just when I thought I was out of the Tilt-a-Whirl woods, what should Adrienne and Nichole spot along the highway but a small town carnival. It had stopped raining alltogether, so there was nothing to do but pull in, walk through the soggy grass and make the best of it.

But a carnival just isn't the same as Six Flags. And even though I held my breath and rode a couple of rides with Nichole, I had to explain to her that I couldn't handle the ones that spun, whirled and churned.

All the way home I could feel Nichole's disappointment. I

wondered what thoughts were running through her mind, and imagined any number: "What kind of dad would he make? He doesn't even know how to get to Six Flags. I bet my dad could have found it blindfolded."

And what was Adrienne thinking? Was she wondering about my limitations and doubting my ability to take over the roles of husband and father?

By the time we drove back into Decatur, I felt my protective covering holding everything and everyone at arm's length.

After that, I began to withdraw emotionally from Adrienne and the girls. Adrienne, detecting my coolness, started withdrawing from me in order to protect herself. I, in turn, felt her pulling back and wrongly interpreted it as "You're right, you wouldn't make a good father" and retreated even further.

After more than a week, I decided I had no choice but to drop my armor. I sat down with Adrienne and began talking about the trip, her feelings, and the girls. Letting my future family see my shortcomings was an important step to our becoming a blended family. We all needed to talk over the expectations we had for one another.

As Adrienne told me her side of things, I realized that while I was entertaining perfect father/husband expectations for myself, she was also having delusions of grandeur about me. What a role expectation I would have had to live up to if Adrienne and I had married the first summer after we met. She wanted someone to help her with the girls on a daily basis, yet worried about the stepparent/stepchild relationship a second marriage would bring. What an ideal situation to marry a counselor! She had a delightful fantasy of sitting back while I easily molded our children into perfect little storybook figures.

My expectations for Adrienne and the girls were also

more closely related to fantasy than reality. Just as a pastor would like to have perfectly angelic, righteous children, a counselor would like to have perfectly healthy, obedient children for credibility's sake.

Other couples experience difficulties for any number of reasons. Here are some to be aware of:

Don't exaggerate your future mate's qualities to your children. Making someone into something he isn't will only force him into a family role he can't fill. Give him a chance to be himself.

Realize the children may have unrealistic expectations of the stepparent. Younger children in particular may expect the stepparent to have all the good qualities of the non-custodial parent, as well as a few from neighbors, acquaintances or super-heroes they see on TV.

Discuss the possibility of custody changes with your future mate. For a variety of reasons custody changes may take place. At the death or serious illness of an ex-mate the non-custodial parent becomes the custodial parent. The children themselves may push for a change in custody. Or the father who lost his family and home may find himself with a new wife, a new home and a new desire to have his children with him.

Don't expect to give and receive love instantly. This line of thinking will only lead to disappointment. Even in our instant society, instant love is not likely. After six years as a stepfather I still have a lot to gain in my relationship with my stepdaughters. The transition from stranger to confidant takes time and patience. Many natural parents feel they have yet "to arrive"; how much more so do stepparents!

It is possible that you or your mate may not be able to relate well to the children in the blended family and may not experience closeness. Don't push. Accept the level at which your family can relate and be willing to build on what you do have.

Trying to construct a blended family on unrealistic expectations is like trying to hang a bell in a belfry before laying the foundation of the church. The messy, muddy, unglorified work of digging footings, mixing mortar and laying the bricks must come first.

Where do I fit in?

The second foundation stone for a solid marriage involves the children and their needs.

While you and your future mate are asking and answering questions, the children may have a few of their own. Children may not verbalize their questions, however, because either they don't know how to ask them, or they are afraid of offending one of the adults. And some children may anticipate an answer they don't want to hear. When these children finally express their questions, they sound like an angry attack.

In order to reduce the children's anxieties and help them in the transition, try to reassure them as much as possible, and answer such questions as these, even if they aren't being asked:

> How often will I see Dad (or Mom)?
> Where am I going to live?
> Will I still see my grandma and grandpa?
> What will my last name be?
> Will Uncle Charlie still be my uncle?
> Will Dad still come to my ballgames?
> Will you have time for me?

Even if you've answered these questions a thousand

times, keep on answering. There are legitimate reasons why a child will ask the same questions over and over. He could be too young in his developmental level to comprehend what is being said. Or he may not want to accept it. If he tunes out the answer, whether consciously or unconsciously, he doesn't have to deal with it. Or it could be that even though he has the information, he is as anxious as ever and needs to be reassured over and over.

When Laura and Al began dating, Laura's three-year-old son by her first marriage grew accustomed to having Al visit in the evening and then go home. Laura patiently explained to Steven that she and Al were going to be married and that meant that Al would be living with them.

The first night back home after a brief honeymoon, Laura and Al were sitting on the sofa, cozy and talking in low voices when a little blond head bobbed around the corner.

Seeing the quizzical look on her son's face, Laura asked, "What is it, Steven? Why aren't you asleep?"

Steven looked up at her and asked, "When is Al going home?"

Laura explained the situation to him again. "Honey, he isn't going home. Al and I are married and he lives here now."

"Oh," he nodded, turned and padded back to bed.

Laura had used good foresight in answering Steven's questions before her marriage to Al. However, when the talk became fact, Steven still needed to have it explained to him. Laura would have had a more difficult time trying to explain it that evening if she had not prepared Steven in advance.

You can't offer too much reassurance—both before and after the wedding. Children need to be reassured that you will respect their relationship with their non-custodial parent, that you will try to minimize changes in visitation after your new marriage, and that you will still have time for them.

The Couple Relationship

I can't begin to count the number of young people I have talked to who wished their parents would divorce. We are often so concerned about the effects of divorce we overlook the effects on children being reared in a family where fighting between parents is the norm.

What I consider to be one of the most important commodities in a nuclear family is equally important in a blended family. This is the third foundation stone: A husband and wife must have a deep, mature and resilient love for one another. It is the quality of this relationship that is a major contributor to the emotional climate in the home.

I remember a scene in a movie in which a new secretary falls prey to a computerized copy machine. Calmly, the secretary walks to the copy machine, puts in her material to be copied, punches a few buttons and waits. For a few moments, nothing. Then, with a great whir and hum, the copy machine lights up and promptly begins spewing out papers in double time. As she grabs frantically at the sheets, she hears the click of the collator and turns helplessly to watch it shuffle, sort and stack. The velocity with which it works causes new stacks of paper to blow around the room. She scrambles wildly trying to catch papers in mid-air when her supervisor walks into the room, tries to yell above the din, then hurries to the machine and flips a switch marked "Off."

Parents in single parent households often describe the same overwhelming feeling in their lives: running around helplessly as their children fly out of control. There are three specific barriers that seem to prevent them from finding the "off" button. The first is the fear of losing their children's love. "If I tell them they can't do something, they may get angry at me." The second barrier is fear of rebellion. "If I tell them they can't do something, they may do it—and more!" The third is guilt. "I ruined my children's lives by getting a divorce. I deserve to have them treat me badly."

But a new mate in a good marital relationship can help provide the love, strength and understanding the biological parent may need in order to flip the "off" switch. The biological parent, in turn, can help the new mate feel secure in his new position. They can work together for the benefit of the children. Although some parents feel they are betraying their children by forming a close, loving relationship with their new spouses, it is the very best thing they can do.

Dealing with problems quickly, honestly and openly builds a stronger marriage. And by becoming better mates, you will become better parents.

Children and Marriage Plans

David got a new stepfather completely by surprise. He went to stay with his grandmother one weekend and had no idea of his mother's plans to remarry. Then when David returned home and walked through his front door, duffle bag in tow, he was met by a strange man and his mother's quick introduction: "Neal, this is David. David, this is Neal, your new dad."

Even though this seems extreme, it does happen, and illustrates the need for the fourth foundation stone in building a strong new family: Include the children in the wedding and family plans. Otherwise, like David, children may feel that they don't count in family matters and that they have no control over their lives. It is important for children's feelings of self-worth and security to be included in their natural parents' marriage plans.

Nichole and Jennifer were more than happy to help Adrienne and me with our wedding plans and to participate in the ceremony. They helped Adrienne shop for patterns and material for dresses and ran all over town looking for just the right shade of silk flowers and gifts for the attendants. The four of us looked at wedding cakes (they insisted nothing but eight layers would do), and the girls even helped Adrienne and a friend make mints, dozens and dozens of peach and blue mints.

At the rehearsal dinner Jennifer made the comment, "Tomorrow we marry Dad," and still refers to our wedding as "the day we all got married." Whenever we pull out the family album and turn to the wedding pictures, the girls are in them.

Being included made them feel like important members of our new family and lessened their anxiety about the changes they were soon to experience because of our marriage. They came to realize our commitment to one another and to them, and that I was a very special person to their mother and the three of them were very special to me.

If a wedding service has already been conducted and the children were not included, couples may want to ask a pastor to officiate at a special service to dedicate the blended family to the Lord. Parents can also include the children in anniversary celebrations, remembering it as the day the family joined together. Couples can celebrate part of the day with the children and have a special celebration time for themselves.

Territory

Territory and respect for children's possessions is some-times overlooked as a necessary foundation stone. Yet what an issue! Small children don't want to share their toys. Teens don't want to share their space. Mother doesn't want to share her kitchen. And Dad doesn't want to share his workbench. When you have "your" territory, you fight to keep it. When you don't have any territory, you fight to get it.

Complaints from children range from the serious to the seemingly superficial. Here is a sampling of what parents may hear their children say:

"You may have lived here before I did, but my Dad's paying the bills."

"That's my closet, my bulletin board, my bathroom, my hair dryer, my soap dish and my Dixie cup dispenser."

"Mother, Sandra rearranged the bedroom while I was gone. Moving into my bedroom doesn't give her squatters rights. Tell her to put everything back the way I had it."

"Dad, tell Jerry that was our TV before he moved in, and I get to watch what I want to watch."

Fighting for territory in a blended family is more intense than finding your own little niche in a nuclear family. Be-cause the bonding between biological siblings is absent, stepsiblings need to be assured they are not going to be taken advantage of. They need to know that both the biolog-ical parent and the stepparent are going to do the best they can to make everything territorially fair.

This doesn't necessarily mean everyone will be happy with the new living arrangements; most changes will be a compromise from what you really want to what is realistically available. Buying a new home with separate bedrooms for each child is not always a financial option for blended families. And often two biological sisters (or brothers) have to give up their separate bedrooms and share to make room for a new little brother (or sister), complaining that the stepsibling gets a room to himself.

As parental figures you need to keep three things in mind.

First, we all need our "space"—some little corner to call our own. Second, we all need our "stuff"—possessions which are ours alone. And third, parents need to guarantee that the children's "space" and "stuff" will be respected and protected. Children who only come for the weekend have the same territorial needs. Their feeling of being "at home" will be aided by having some of their stuff in their space.

So look at floor plans. Plan living arrangements. Talk over respect for personal property. Working with children well in advance of a remarriage does not guarantee a smooth territory transition, but it will certainly facilitate it.

A Picture of the Future

I have met biological and stepparents alike who have resigned themselves to "just making it." These parents fail to recognize that although external situations affect us, they do not have to control us. Our controls are internal; we decide on the quality of life we are going to have. When you accept responsibility for your family life, you bring to it purposeful direction. When you do not accept responsibility, the controls become external, based on circumstances.

Try this exercise. You and your spouse each write a letter—just like those informative family letters we have all received from relatives at Christmas—describing how you would like your lives to be five years into the future. Include such things as:

How your family is doing
What each family member is involved in
How you get along with your children's other
      biological parent
Family and individual relationships with exténded
      family members
How your neighbors would describe your family
The education level of each family member
Particulars in regard to careers
Who your family friends are and what they are like
Where your family and individual family
      members are spiritually and how they
      maintain their spiritual lives
Family health, including athletic involvement, diet
      and exercise
How much your family earns, how it is spent and
      invested
What you do as a family for entertainment
What you do as a couple for entertainment

Write this letter as if it were a dream or fantasy. Imagine every decision you made was the right one. Whether you imagined you bought a new house, stayed in your current residence or moved out of town, you made the right decision.

After you have written your individual letters, sit down together and incorporate them. Make sure you both state everything in positive terms. Remember this is a dream, a fantasy. Don't limit yourselves.

Once you have decided where you want to be in five

years, you need to ask yourselves questions like what you will have to accomplish each year and what you need to do today to reach your five-year-dream.

The purpose of this letter is threefold. It gives you an idea of what you are hoping for, it helps you visualize where you are headed and, most importantly, it is a step toward controlling today's behavior by setting goals.

Suppose someone walked up to you today and said, "Here's two thousand dollars. Go buy yourself some clothes." Your shopping choices would be affected by your future plans.

If I see myself at this time next year still in private practice, writing and teaching seminars, I would go out and buy a couple of suits and sport jackets, and spend the rest of the money on slacks, white shirts and ties. If, however, I see myself as a back-to-basics teacher, gardener, farmer and therapist living on a farm with a dormhouse for high school boys, I would certainly not buy suits. I would go for blue jeans, flannel shirts and long underwear.

My picture of the future shapes my behavior today. If I believe that in five years my family life will be unhappy, difficult and antagonistic, my lack of hope and absence of vision will bring out undesirable attitudes in me, and then in my family. It is important to begin seeing your blended family living in harmony together. Look for that potential. Forget what is behind and press on toward the goal of unity. Catch the vision.

3

A Vision of Unity

Every family has a system, a way of operating that is uniquely its own. Quite possibly, we can be too close to the day-by-day family interaction to see the system at work, but it is composed of:

The role each person plays
The emotional climate of the home
The way family members interact with one
       another and with the family as a whole
The expectations each family member has of one
       another
The way individuals fill those expectations
Communication, spoken and unspoken
Traditions and celebrations
Rules and manners
Use of leisure and work time

The family system describes the actions of the family: when they get up, when they go to bed, when they eat, what they eat, how they cook what they eat, what they wear, what they don't wear, how they take care of what they wear, when they watch television, and if they even have a television. The list goes on and on.

Co-Conductors

The family system Adrienne and I developed was much more complicated than an original nuclear family system. We were faced with mixing the influences from Adrienne's and my parents, the family system she had with the girls' biological father, her single-parent system with Nichole and Jennifer, and my system as a bachelor.

Some couples have entered remarriage thinking the blending of their familiies would come naturally, only to find it takes hard work and careful planning.

If blending, or integration, does not take place in a reconstituted family, its members sound like two bands led by two different conductors, playing two different songs in two different keys. I have counseled blended families where each original family system insisted on playing its own song, and on playing it louder and louder in an attempt to drown the other song out. Eventually the original tune gave way to blasting noise and family discord.

A member of one such household, now an adult, told me what it was like when his mother remarried. Until that time, Mike had been the "baby" of the Traxler family; then he found himself sandwiched in between the two Morgan children. In the new stepfamily, neither his mother nor his stepfather was willing to give up the old systems and work into a new, unified family system. Both wanted to be sole conductors.

The invisible dividing line between families started at the dinner table, where the Traxlers sat on one side and the

Morgans the other, and moved into almost every area of family life. For instance, his stepfather's two children were expected to bring home straight A's and be proficient in sports and extracurricular activities, while his mother decided that any grades Mike and his sister brought home were all right, just as long as they were doing their best.

The lack of blending between the parents in rules, guidelines and expectations made it difficult for both sets of children to accept their stepparent's authority. It also produced fierce competition resulting in jealousy and hostility.

Although all the children are now grown with families of their own, they and their parents still do not experience family unity. The parents never entertain the whole family at the same time and the competition between the stepchildren continues.

For blending to take place in a reconstituted family, the new mates must work closely together, analyzing their personal styles, minimizing their weaknesses and maximizing their strengths. With time and lots of practice their blended bands will begin to play a harmonious family melody.

A Token Role Without Control

One of the first steps to accomplishing integration in a blended family is for the new mates to develop a co-conductor system. Before Adrienne and I married, she had to give serious consideration to the changes she would have to make. Talking about changing from a single-parent household system to co-conducting was one thing; actually doing it was another.

Adrienne had just gotten used to being the head of a single-parent household and, although she didn't like being the sole decision-maker, she was used to being the one in control. Our marriage meant she had to be willing to let me have the parental authority I needed in my role as head of the household. She had to trust me enough to run the system she had put together.

All too frequently, the biological parent gives the step-parent "a token role without control." It is not unusual for the biological parent to send a double message to his mate: "I want your help, but I don't want your help." The biological parent may really want his mate to be a co-conductor, but for a variety of reasons won't let it happen.

One reason is that he wants to protect the children from any further pain or emotional upset. Such comments as: "She's too tough on them," or "She just doesn't know what they have been through," are common reactions.

A custodial parent may also fear his children will become angry with the stepparent and want to go live with their other biological parent. The possibility of losing his children's love makes it difficult for a parent to join in co-conducting.

In one stepparent group session, a young mother commented, "It's a little discouraging when you've already messed up your first marriage to find out your new husband is a better parent than you are, and they're not even his kids!" Biological parents feeling this inner threat may find themselves hindering the stepparent's involvement with the children out of fear of further failure. Their thoughts go something like: "I failed as a spouse in my first marriage. If my new spouse is a better parent than I am, I'm a failure as a parent too."

Sandy's double message to her mate was in part due to their different discipline styles. Sandy was very lenient when it came to discipline, while her second husband, Stu, was authoritarian. Sandy brought four boys into their marriage and repeatedly told Stu she wanted him to be a father to her children. Yet each time he stepped in to assume his role, Sandy complained about the way he handled it. She continually blocked his control and discipline in front of the children.

One Saturday morning Sandy complained to Stu about her oldest son's selfishness with the television. Billy's constant switching of channels kept the other boys in an uproar and prevented Sandy from getting her housework done.

Stu responded by calling Billy into the kitchen and telling him sternly, "The next time you flip the station when your brothers are watching a program, you'll be sent to your room."

Not long after, just when Stu was thinking how well he had handled the situation, he heard the boys wrestling again in the family room. Billy, bored with the "baby" cartoons the younger boys were watching, had changed the channel. Stu immediately sent him to his room. Billy ran up the steps in a rage, stomping and slamming doors all the way.

Sandy heard the commotion from the kitchen and came running out to see what was happening. When she heard Stu's explanation, she openly disagreed with him in front of the younger boys.

A few minutes later Stu had to leave the house to run an errand. He had no sooner gone out the door when Billy came strolling into the family room. Sandy, thinking Stu had been too hard on Billy, not only allowed him to watch television, but sent the other boys outside to play in order for Billy to watch any program he wanted.

Stu's errand didn't take long. When he returned home he was furious to find Billy downstairs watching TV. Stu walked angrily into the kitchen, looked at Sandy and shook his head in resignation. "What I think doesn't matter to you, does it? I don't know why I bother to discipline the children, when whatever I do is always wrong."

The double message Sandy was sending Stu was, "You can be in the role of father, but you can't have any authority with it."

Double messages are dangerous. They only serve to divide biological and stepparents and prevent a unified front.

Easing in the Co-Conductor

When an industry has a management position to fill, it generally promotes from within the company. This is usually done because the one in line for promotion has had time to learn from the inside how the system works. Ideally, he goes through an on-the-job training program, easing into the responsibilities, while able to divert major decisions to someone with more experience.

In applying this concept to blended families, we have termed it "easing in the co-conductor." This is an interval for the biological parent to lead in discipline decisions while the new mate eases into the co-management position. During that time, the stepparent primarily supports the rules of the biological parent, while gradually coming into his or her own right as a parent. This accomplishes two things. It allows the stepparent to get to know the system that has been going on for years, and it gives the children time to get to know and accept the stepparent.

Frequently in single-parent households the biological parent becomes overpermissive. When a stepparent arrives on the scene, he may be all too aware of the job that needs to be done and find it difficult to hang back on the sidelines. Jumping in to straighten the new family out, however, while they are still serving the wedding cake will most likely win the stepparent a number of enemies, the new mate included. Trust must come first between mates in the new relationship; then the children must be made aware that authority has been delegated to the new mate, especially in the absence of the biological parent.

One evening in my early months as a stepfather, I stayed home with the girls while Adrienne went to a baby shower. When bedtime came around I walked into the room where Jennifer and Nichole were playing and announced, "Girls, it's time to get ready for bed."

They sat where they were and continued playing.

"Girls, it's 8:15 and time to get ready for bed."

Still no response.

"Nichole and Jennifer, it's time for bed *now.*"

Then, without so much as a glance in my direction, Jennifer remarked, "You're not our boss."

During the ensuing silence I fought off the impulse to challenge Jennifer's statement. Instead I replied calmly but firmly, "Jennifer, your mother told me to have you and Nichole in bed by 8:30 and that is what I am going to do." After a moment both girls said, "Oh," and began getting ready for bed.

When they understood that I was following their mother's instructions, they responded according to their relationship with her. Initially they obeyed me, not because they loved and respected me, but because they respected their mom.

Somewhere between a year and a half and two years (which we found out later is the norm), I no longer needed to rely on Adrienne's relationship with the girls to establish my parental responsibilities in the family. I had achieved the status of co-conductor through my own parental relationship with Nichole and Jennifer.

Blended Families Are Not Nuclear Families

One wrong assumption—that blended families are like original nuclear families with just a few more people here and there—can be hazardous to your mental health. Blended families have a more complex family structure and extra problems which seem to descend from nowhere.

Striving to mold a blended family into a nuclear family system leads to frustration and chronic unhappiness for all its members. Accepting your blended family as different from your original family dream will release you to move ahead and make the very best of the family you are in.

Sharon's five-year-old son, Danny, began to feel some of the strains of having two sets of parents. When Danny first returned home after visiting his father and stepmother for two weeks, he followed his mother everywhere, hanging on her and not wanting her to go anywhere without him. When his father came to pick him up the following Friday for another visit, Danny ran to his bedroom and hid. His father decided to give him more time to adjust and, rather than pressing the issue, left without him.

Sharon waited for the right moment to talk with Danny. One evening while she was setting the table, she asked him what he was thinking so hard about.

After a few moments silence, he answered, "I want just one mommy and one daddy."

Sharon pulled out a chair and sat Danny on her lap.

"What about Pop?" she asked, refering to Danny's step-father. "What would we do with him?"

"Well, Pop would just have to find another wife."

"But Danny, that would make me very unhappy. I love Pop and would really miss him."

Danny looked perplexed a moment, then his face lit up. "I

know. You can be my one mommy and Pop can be my one daddy."

Sharon wanted to say, "O.K., Danny. No problem. We'll do just that and we'll all live happily ever after, you and me and Pop." What she did say was, "Danny, you have your father and Amy and me and Pop. Just think, instead of having only two people to love you, you have four."

That seemed to do the trick. After their talk Danny was calmer and less anxious. If Sharon had shown anger or frustration at the whole situation, it could have made Danny oversensitive to having four parental figures. Instead, she was careful to help Danny accept being part of two households. As Sharon related this story to us, she shared how surprised she was at her own willingness to accept her current circumstances.

Children coming and going between two separate households is typical of the blended family system. Nowhere in Adrienne's original family dream did she picture her children leaving one day every weekend and spending an occasional long weekend in another household. Adrienne and I had to accept the fact that there was another household involved in our family system which the girls were very much a part of, while we were not.

In the first months of our family life it confused me how well the girls and I could get along during the week, only to have difficulties when they returned after a weekend stay in their other household. Then it dawned on me: Nichole and Jennifer were just making adjustments to the different rules, standards and systems in their two households.

Working on family unity with one set of children moving between two households can be a struggle. Working on family unity with two sets of children and a *third* household seems impossible. Just trying to keep a schedule of which set will be home when is mind-boggling.

Couples have shared with us how their family unity suffers when non-custodial children arrive for the weekend. Bruce and Marsha, for instance, changed their roles and rules every other weekend, making everyone, including the non-custodial children, feel out of kilter. "Marsha and I completely turned our relationship off when my three boys came to visit. I became the children's entertainer, while Marsha became chief cook and bottle-washer."

Changing roles and rules whenever children come to spend the day, weekend, week or month is costly to family unity. The children coming for the weekend converge on the house like little tyrants. The children residing there become aggressive and hostile. The wife may lock herself in the bathroom while the husband wanders around the house mumbling, "One little, two little, three little Indians, four little, five. . . ."

Including all of the children in the family program, whether they are custodial or non-custodial, is essential for family unity. Part of this process requires psychologically accepting non-custodial children as your children and not "visitors." A number of stepparents have gone into marriage thinking the non-custodial children will not affect their lives only to discover they are a very integral part of the family system.

Some stepparents and even biological parents view their children's visits as something to be endured. "So what if little Johnny is a self-appointed comptroller of the TV set and Sarah polished off a one-pound package of Snickers this morning. We can always buy more candy bars. They're not here very often and they'll be gone soon."

Accepting the non-custodial child as a permanent member of your family system, with its rules and standards, can be difficult for both the biological and stepparent. Becoming closely attached to someone who has to leave at the end of every weekend, whose life you feel you have no control over and whose love you fear losing, is tough; but it is much tougher for everyone involved to live a lifestyle of wishing for the weekend to be over.

The Risks of Changing

Many times people walk into my office complaining they are hurting. Together we work out a program to help them live a more effective lifestyle to remove some of that hurting; but then they refuse to follow the program. To these people the risk involved in change might hurt even more than the current situation. Willingness to change leaves all of us open to growth—which sounds reasonable. Yet the thing we must be willing to change is not so much our environment but ourselves—which sounds very unreasonable.

When I married Adrienne, I had to change my single lifestyle to that of family man.

No longer was I able to take off with friends on the spur of the moment. There was the sometimes insurmountable task of finding a babysitter. Then, after finding a sitter, we couldn't stay out very late because Adrienne worried about getting the sitter home at a decent hour.

I am a night person with my energy level peaking at midnight. To my dismay, I discovered Adrienne and the girls are morning people with their energy levels peaking at six a.m. With Adrienne rattling pans in the kitchen, Jennifer and Nichole wrestling in their bedroom or running up and down the hall, and Fred, the dog, barking at every thump on the wall or bump on the floor, sleeping in seemed like a dream of the past.

I no longer ate when I was hungry. I ate when the children were hungry. I no longer got the best cut of meat. I ate what was left when the plate was passed.

And I wasn't the only one suffering. I liked Adrienne's company in the evening and wanted her to stay up with me. The first few months she complied, until she became so grumpy during the day, I begged her to go to bed early. The girls were no longer allowed to run in and out of our bedroom any time of the day or night. They all had to give up their favorite TV programs one night a week for my Monday night football. Even Fred had to make changes. His sleeping quarters moved from the foot of our bed, to a beanbag in the corner of our bedroom, to the hallway and finally to the girls' room. The issue in our adjusting to one another as a family was not really the changes we made, but our willingness to make them.

Some changes can be forced, with everyone gritting his teeth because of them. I could have gone into the family room, turned on the football game and announced gruffly, "Girls, from now on this is my night to watch TV. If you don't like it, you can go upstairs." They would have gone upstairs angry, wondering, "Who does he think he is, anyway?" Instead we all came to an agreement that Monday night was my night for football.

The early riser versus the night owl did not work out quite as congenially. Adrienne expected me to jump out of bed, fling the window open, crow with the roosters and still be able to function the rest of the day. Much to her chagrin, I have never viewed getting up in the morning as a high point in my day. I made it a practice to never get out of bed until the last possible minute.

Adrienne did everything she could think of to get me up. On her more subdued mornings she left the door open for me to hear any and every sound she, the girls, or Fred would make. I woke up but we all wound up grouchy.

The more she insisted I needed to get out of bed earlier, the later I would sleep, until finally she gave up. With one grand statement she acquiesced. "Tom, you sleep as late as you want. Far be it from me to stop you from sleeping your life away if that's what you really want to do."

The next morning when the girls woke up, Adrienne fed them breakfast and told them to play quietly downstairs. She didn't come back to the bedroom every five minutes to see if I was up. As a matter of fact, she didn't come back to wake me at all and I loved it. And once she stopped trying to force me to be an early bird, something very strange began to happen. I started wanting to get up earlier. And even stranger, I did. When Adrienne quit trying to change me, I had the motivation to change myself. And the turmoil between us, which caught the girls in the crossfire, ended.

Accepting Differences

Have you ever counted all of the things your stepchildren do wrong in one morning? They don't say good morning. They put too much water in the bathtub. They squeeze the toothpaste from the center of the tube instead of rolling it neatly from the bottom up. They don't flip the bedspread over their pillows when they make their beds. They always turn the radio on too loud and never turn it off. They gobble their cereal and slurp their orange juice. They never put the sugar bowl back in the cupboard. They scrape their metal lunchboxes across the counter when they pick them up. When they leave for school they slam the door, leaving the windows and your teeth clattering.

Now the question is: Did they really do all of those things wrong? Or are you intolerant of differences? One step-mother, realizing that her intolerance might have been a big reason she was having difficulty with her stepson, concluded, "If my son and my stepson were both in the same room doing the same thing, my stepson would get on my nerves while my son wouldn't. And the same thing is true for my husband. My son would get on his nerves while his son wouldn't." Her example shows the level of acceptance of the biological parent, not the wrongness of the stepchild.

These minor differences turn into major irritations when they become a focal point in the stepparent/stepchild relationship. I have discovered that the list of behaviors parents focus on is endless. When I have asked stepparents, "What is the one thing that really bothers you about your stepchild?" I have heard everything from "the way she takes off her make-up" to "the way he walks."

Because of the close quarters at mealtime (if the family is still eating together), table manners enter the spotlight. Since this is such an issue in stepfamilies, I have made up the following Table Tolerance Quiz. Check the items over which you are willing to dissolve family harmony.

_____ 1. Napkin is not on lap.
_____ 2. Uses both hands instead of leaving one hand in lap while eating.
_____ 3. Comes to the dinner table without a shirt.
_____ 4. Clicks teeth with fork.
_____ 5. Chews with mouth open.
_____ 6. Slurps drink or soup.
_____ 7. Eats with elbows on the table.
_____ 8. Poor posture.
_____ 9. Uses fingers as eating utensils.
_____ 10. Burps at the table.
_____ 11. Slips food to Fido under the table.
_____ 12. Says "Yuck" or "Gross" after seeing what's for supper.

_____ 13. Eats only preferred foods instead of some of everything.

_____ 14. Won't clean plate but expects dessert.

_____ 15. Makes disgusting noises or is disruptive while eating.

_____ 16. Holds knife and fork like daggers or spoon like a shovel.

_____ 17. Spills milk.

_____ 18. Does not wait until everyone is seated and prayer is said before starting to eat.

_____ 19. Scrapes margarine off the top rather than off the end.

_____ 20. Talks during mealtime.

_____ 21. Leaves the table without asking to be excused.

_____ 22. Talks on the phone during mealtime.

To discover which table tolerance category you fit into, count the number of items you checked and find the corresponding number below.

3 or fewer:	The children won't let _you_ eat at the table.
4-7:	Your motto is, "Peace at any price."
8-12:	Average. (This is where Adrienne and I scored, so you must be O.K.!)
13-17:	A little picky?
18-21:	You believe that breaking the person is better than breaking the rules.

Most of the behaviors listed above are things you may want to teach your children but are they worth disrupting family unity? When Adrienne and I were first married I probably would have scored a solid 17 or 18 on the Table Tolerance Quiz. After several mealtime disasters, Adrienne was able to convince me my expectations were a little high and my lecturing was not working.

Thanks to Dr. James Dobson and his "Focus on the Family" film series, we found a system we call the "napkin count" that does work. The four of us sat down together and made a list of good table manners. The consequence for breaking one of the rules is to leave the table, run to the bathroom and count to twenty loudly and slowly enough for everyone to hear. Nichole and Jennifer have as much opportunity to send me in for the "countdown" as I have to send them. Now, instead of the girls feeling like I am always finding fault with them, the whole family is working toward better table manners.

There are areas in life made up of definite rights and wrongs, but there are many more where the answer lies in how you were taught.

If a stepmother was trained to dry the dishes as soon as the dishwater is emptied from the sink and her stepdaughter was taught to let the dishes airdry in the drainer, a conflict may result. If a stepson always washes the outside of the car first, and his stepfather was taught to clean the inside first, who is to say which one is right? There are many ways to do everything. Willingness to accept the differences is a key to family unity.

Blended Family Survival Kit

There are some basic tactics for surviving in the wilderness of stepparenting and for bringing unity to a fragmented family system. The following survival strategies are usually acquired by the original nuclear family over a period of time, but for a blended family they are an immediate necessity.

Courtesy. Undoubtedly, the major culprit of disrespect is the tongue. "The tongue is small, yet full of boasting. Behold it can set a whole house on fire with just a small spark" (James 3:5, Frydenger paraphrase). The way family members speak to each other sets the course towards unity or constant, heated arguments. The following "thou shalt nots" should be observed by every member of the family.

> Thou shalt not yell.
> Thou shalt not engage in name-calling.
> Thou shalt not talk back.
> Thou shalt not make sarcastic, derogatory or cutting remarks.

One summer the girls picked up the bad habit of adding the word dummy to their sisterly conversations: "Why did you do that, dummy?" or "Hey, *dummy*, Mom wants you to clean out the bathroom sink."

We informed the girls that, contrary to what we were hearing around the house, we were not the parents of twin dummies and we were going to impose consequences for name-calling. Whenever they used the word dummy they were to put a dime in the family kitty. If they were dimeless, or if name-calling was a result of anger or an argument, they had ten-minute reservations in Corners A and B of the living room.

It is easy to see the escalating anger that can come from yelling or name-calling. The silent treatment, on the other hand, is less openly hostile but equally damaging. Treating someone to silence is saying, "You are a non-person," and is another form of disrespect.

Become aware of what is happening in your home in terms of respect or disrespect. Observe your children's behavior and take note of their individual displays of courtesy or lack of respect. It helps to devise consequences for disrespectful behavior and rewards for courteous behavior.

Respect is best learned by parental modeling. Ask your children, "Are there things I do or don't do that make you feel I don't respect you?" or for younger children, "Do I ever hurt your feelings? How?" Ask your mate, "What are the ways in which I show respect or disrespect for you or the children?" Remember, if you yell or resort to name-calling, so will your children. If you exercise the Golden Rule of "doing unto others as you would have them do unto you," you will find that God's promise of sowing and reaping will operate in your home.

Basic Ground Rules. Basic ground rules cover fundamental areas such as personal hygiene, moral values, respect for authority, respect for property and social laws. If basic ground rules are not set up and communicated to children, they will not know what the limits really are. When children do not know the limits, any behavior is possible.

The following questions may be helpful to you in setting up the ground rules for your blended family.

> What time is curfew?
> When can teenage children use the family car?
> What is the time limit on the telephone?
> What are television privileges?
> Will the children receive an allowance? If so, how much?
> What happens when chores are not completed?
> What are the bare essentials of personal hygiene?
> What is appropriate dress around the house?
> Who is allowed in the house when parents are not there?
> What happens if a child skips school?
> How will dishonesty be dealt with?

What about coarse or vulgar language?
What action will be taken if a child smokes, drinks
      or uses drugs?
Are children expected to obey the laws of the land?
What are the consequences for damaging personal
      property?

Leonard's household had almost no rules when he met Kay. His first wife had been ill and had difficulty caring for their four children and keeping up with housework. After her death Leonard went into a deep depression, leaving his four children to care for themselves for several more years.

Leonard's children were sixteen, fourteen, thirteen and eleven when he proposed marriage to Kay. They did not have a curfew. They ate whenever and wherever they wanted. They went to bed late and got up when they felt like it. They had no concept of what it meant to work for an allowance. Leonard, feeling guilty over neglecting them for so long, gave them money whenever they asked for it. They had no qualms about tramping through the house with mud-or snow-caked boots. Avoiding soap and water at all costs had become an unwritten canon. Every piece of furniture was damaged in one way or another, and the oldest son would leave his cigarette butts where he put them out and the ashes where they fell.

Before Kay was willing to marry Leonard and move into his home, she wanted some basic rules established. Leonard was willing to do anything to get his life and his children back in order. He sat down with Kay and together they set up appropriate ground rules—and stuck to them.

They started with the basics and began moving the children toward maturity one step at a time. As the children became more accustomed to the structure they never had,

Leonard and Kay were able to add more responsibilities and trust the children to accept them.

Fairness. When Jerry and Alice came to me seeking counseling, they discussed Alice's feeling of being overworked both at home and at the office. She explained, "I'm worn out trying to juggle my job and household responsibilities. Any free time I have is spent cooking, cleaning or washing clothes."

After a lengthy discussion it was decided Alice didn't have much control over her work situation, but she and Jerry could control what was happening at home. For starters, if each of their four children (three hers, one his) picked up his own mess and helped out with the household chores, Alice's work load would lighten considerably.

This appeared to be a simple solution—until they began to distribute the chores among the children. They agreed on the chores to be done by Alice's sixteen-, fourteen-and ten-yearold, but disagreed over the work to be done by Jerry's sixteen-year-old daughter, Tina.

"Alice," Jerry insisted, "you know Tina has a job. She shouldn't have to do any chores beyond taking care of her room."

"That isn't fair," Alice countered. "None of the money she makes goes for clothing, school supplies, school lunches, bus fare or anything else that would save the family money. And to top it off, you insist on giving her an allowance because my children get one." She continued, "Tina has a later curfew, she's allowed more privileges than any of the other children and you never call her on the carpet for misbehaving."

Bingo! We had hit the real sore spot: unfairness toward the children.

Alice was angry at Jerry's unwillingness to require Tina to

help around the house and follow household rules. She reasoned that if Tina wasn't going to do anything, she wasn't about to make her children do anything either; so Alice was overworked, overwrought and resentful.

The solution for Alice and Jerry is one many blended family couples must institute. Set identical rules for all the children, custodial and non-custodial. What's good for the goose's goslings is good for the gander's. Of course this does not mean the five-year-old can do everything the sixteen-year-old can. Rules must be based on a child's age and level of maturity. The distance Jennifer was allowed to ride her bicycle at age five was not nearly as far as she could ride at age eight.

If you have two children the same age, the rules may start out alike, but may change should one child continually obey them while the other child chooses to ignore them. It would be unfair to tighten Billy's curfew because his stepsister constantly comes home late and is being penalized. Although the same basic rules should be set up for all the children, each child should be recognized for his own behavior and attitudes.

The clearer the rules, the better the chances for them to be fair. And both the biological parent and stepparent must agree to follow the rules they have established.

Division of Labor. Much resentment arises in a blended family due to the way household work has or has not been divided up. When the children of one parent feel they are doing more than their stepbrothers or stepsisters, they become angry. If a stepmother cannot get Dad's backing concerning his children's help around the house she begins to feel like a maid instead of a mate. A stepfather may become jealous of the time Mom spends doing everything for her children. Or everybody becomes resentful because no one is doing anything.

Blended family parents may want to keep three questions in mind: What will make the family system flow better? How can everybody participate fairly? How can we keep bitterness and resentment from growing?

There is more value to household chores than just keeping resentment from growing. They help children feel like a part of the family system. When Jennifer and Nichole come home from spending time with their father and stepmother, they often tell us how much fun they had helping mow the yard, work in the garden, cook supper or vacuum. Part of that enjoyment comes from doing something other than the same old boring chores Adrienne and I have assigned, but it also makes them feel they are an important part of their other household and can contribute to it, which makes helping a reward in itself.

It has been my experience that children who are responsible for daily chores at home are generally more responsible in their academic work as well. They have learned the discipline of applying themselves on a daily basis.

Chores in our home fall into two categories: personal chores and family chores. Personal chores include anything related to personal hygiene: making beds, cleaning bedrooms, hanging up clothes. Family chores are directed toward the well-being of the family: dusting, vacuuming, mowing the yard, setting the table.

As a general rule of thumb every family member should have from 15 to 30 minutes (depending on age) of family chores assigned every day. The time allotted for each chore is based on how long it would take one of the parents to complete it while working at a moderate pace. I have seen my girls do their chores in half the time when they have some place they want to go in a hurry, or take more than an hour when they don't want to do them at all. Whatever the time they take, the chore must be done up to standard before it is considered completed.

Chores should be distributed at the family meeting, partly by volunteering and partly by parental assignment.[1]

Family Meetings. As children grow older, and especially in adolescent years, they want to feel they have some input into the family decision-making process. This does not mean they begin to control the family or even that they want to, but that they desire to share in decisions that will affect them.

One vehicle for sharing in decision-making is the family meeting. It provides a sense of family continuity, unity and communication. In the last few years even large companies have gone to family meetings, calling them Quality Circles. During these meetings, employees at every level, including management, discuss ways of improving plant operations. Management has discovered it cannot always be aware of everything that is going on and needs the input of front-line employees. In the same way, family meetings allow parents (the management) to get input from their children, with the same respect shown for the youngest as for the oldest and for the custodial as for the non-custodial children.

We make mention of family meetings in this chapter because of their importance in promoting family unity. In Chapter 9 we will discuss family meetings in depth.

Above All

The most important step toward unity is allowing God's presence into blended family relationships. Interaction be-

[1]For more information on family chores see;
Systematic Training for Effective Parenting (STEP) by Don Dinkmeyer and Gary D. McKay, and *Making Children Mind Without Losing Yours* by Dr. Kevin Leman.

tween family members can be compared to a piston within a cylinder wall. A piston runs smoothly when there is adequate oil in the cylinder. When oil is absent, the cylinder quickly overheats, locks and becomes immobile. Blended family relationships can become sticky, hot and immobile without the lubricating oil of the Holy Spirit. Love, joy, peace, patience, kindness, goodness, faithfulness, gentleness and self-control are spiritual lubricants that reduce friction and free your blended family to operate and relate with greater unity.

4

Children Reacting

"Mom, I really miss Simon."

Adrienne stopped sorting through the ornaments and looked up at little Nichole standing by the Christmas tree. Clutching the homemade ornament bearing her cat's name, Nichole was blinking back tears without much success.

"Why, Nichole, I didn't realize you were so attached to Simon. He was getting old and grouchy and wouldn't let you or anyone else near him the last year we had him."

"But, Mom, I miss him. I wish he were here."

All the blinking Nichole could muster didn't stop the torrent of tears that followed.

While trying to comfort her, Adrienne silently attempted to piece together exactly what was happening. As she told me later, she had anticipated a reaction from Nichole when the ornaments with her dad's name came out of the box, but she certainly didn't expect tears over Simon.

Nichole apparently didn't play with Simon much from the time he grew from a kitten into a cat. Then he had been moved into the garage for "marking his territory" all over the house, so she had even less contact with him. When he

58

started leaving territorial markers in the garage, Adrienne decided it was time to give him away. There were a few "Aw, Mom's" from Nichole, but no real protests.

When Adrienne and I talked it over later, she shook her head. "I can't believe Nichole has all those emotions for that cat. She didn't play with Simon, she didn't feed him and she didn't miss him when he was gone."

As we talked we both came to the conclusion that her tears probably were not for Simon, but for her biological father. Simon had been given away just a couple months prior to her parents separation. Nichole's heartbreak was not solely for a black cat, but for the loss of the daily parent-child contact she had had with her father, her nuclear family and the traditions they had all celebrated together.

Mourning Losses

Children's expressions of loss may catch parents completely by surprise just when blended family life seems to be running smoothly: You have a new home in a nice neighborhood, the school system is fine, the church friendly, and there are plenty of children on the block. Everything is great, except that your five-year-old whines all the time, your ten-year-old mopes around and bugs you with questions about the future, and you find yourself asking, "What's going on here?"

What's going on is the experience of loss. Elisabeth Kubler-Ross discovered five emotional stages—denial, anger, bargaining, depression and acceptance—that were experienced by people who knew they were dying. These five stages have since been used to identify what individuals experience with any major loss in their lives. Children of divorced parents, facing emotional struggles, can and do go through these five stages.

When a child has not accepted the reality of the divorce he is in the denial stage. The absent parent is seen as temporarily living someplace else, but still a member of the nuclear family. If one of his parents remarries, the child is tempted to sabotage the new marriage by reasoning, "How can there be a new marriage when Dad and Mom still belong to each other?"

The denial stage is a difficult stage to deal with because the child, by denying the facts, won't discuss them. Don't attack him or overwhelm him with the truth. Don't sit him down and try to change his mind for him. But when he makes incorrect statements, let him know his error. Be consistent about pointing out the truth in a loving, unhurried manner.

While denial is one of the more difficult stages, anger is one of the more challenging. As with Jason, a young man I counseled, anger occurs when reality begins to set in. Jason became a belligerent young man following his parents' divorce and his mother's remarriage. He was striking out not only at his parents, but at teachers, friends and any other adults who showed concern for him. He got into trouble at school repeatedly, his grades fell and he blamed everyone and everything for his difficulties. Through counseling Jason came to realize he was full of anger, and that his anger was there because his father was not.

It is important for children in this stage to deal with their feelings. While most people can identify that they are angry, few know where the anger is really coming from. This is especially the case with children. They need the opportunity to talk about their feelings and understand why they have them. It is also important for the biological parent and stepparent to realize why their child is angry, instead of becoming defensive and angry at the child.

The bargaining stage is familiar to most of us: "God, if

you will do this for me, I will do this for you." In the same way, children engage in spiritual bargaining for parental reunion. The basic idea is, "If I am good, God will put my parents back together."

Sometimes a child will ask, "Hey Mom, if you were ever single again do you think you'd date Dad?" Even if you would, say no. Don't give your child false hope. The last marriage is over. This one is forever.

When a child realizes that bargaining is not going to work and that he is powerless to change his parents' decision, depression sets in. He begins to mourn his loss. It is important not to rush a child through this stage. It is, necessary, however, to reassure him, listen to him and help him express his feelings.

Loss through the death of a parent is a different experience for children than the loss of a daily parent/child relationship through divorce. In divorce there is still contact with the other biological parent. Even if a parent is absent with minimal or no contact, the children always have the hope they will find the absent parent. Death, on the other hand, is final.

In the fifth stage of the loss process, children who have experienced loss through death accept their parent's death, while children who have experienced loss through divorce accept the death of their nuclear family and give up their dream of what might have been.

This final stage may be long in coming. You may be well into your second marriage before your child accepts your divorce, remarriage and new blended family. It is at this point a child decides, basically, "I can't change or control my parents' lives. It doesn't matter how wonderful or how terrible I act. I can't put their marriage back together. I'm just going to have to learn to live with it."

Even though children will express all of the emotions

related to loss, they do not always experience them in sequence. They may drift from one stage to another and back again. This sporadic movement between stages may be due in part to the children's inability to share their sense of loss with the parent. In death, the biological parent can go through the loss process with his children. This is not the case in divorce.

Because of animosity between their parents or loyalty conflicts, children find it difficult to relate their loss comfortably to either parent. If children watch their biological parents fight and bicker (even after divorce and remarriage), they can even re-experience the initial trauma of the loss and return to earlier stages. Biological parents must *willingly decide* to cooperate with one another for their children's best interest.

Development Levels

Just as children react differently to loss and its five stages, they also react differently to divorce and remarriage depending upon their ages and developmental levels. These factors determine a child's needs (whether it is to be cuddled or to express independence) and how he perceives his environment. The following breakdown according to age and developmental level provides an outline which can help you understand your children's behavior.

Infant: Up to 2 Years. Jennifer was sixteen months old when her father and Adrienne separated. Her primary need as an infant was for Adrienne to be emotionally and psychologically secure. Infants are sensitive to the emotional environment produced by their primary caretaker, who is usually the mother.

Even though Mom may be going through all of the right

actions of diapering, feeding, bathing and dressing her baby, if she is a mess emotionally, her baby will be affected by it. For instance, an infant reacts to how his caretaker responds to his coos, smiles and jibberish. If a baby musters up a big smile for Mom and Mom bursts into tears because Dad isn't around to see it, the baby can't help but become confused.

Infants need a great deal of cuddling, touching and loving. Jennifer expressed her need for cuddling by initiating it, making it easy for Adrienne and me to respond to her. Other infants may not be as demonstrative, but they have the same needs.

Preschool: 2-5 Years. Preschoolers, like infants, are very sensitive to their parents' feelings. Their difficulty in handling the absence of one parent and the changes that have taken place in remarriage may show up in their irritability, whining and possible aggression. A parent may also note some examples of regression, such as the five-year-old who always dressed himself, now needing help putting on his clothes, or a potty-trained three-year-old beginning to leave puddles on the floor. Symptoms that appear in this developmental level may take some time to get under control.

Children in this age group may be the most profoundly affected by divorce and remarriage. They have the cognitive ability to understand part of what is going on, but not all, and they cannot adequately express what they are feeling. Even though they are too young to understand fully what is happening, they still need an explanation about the absence of one parent and the possible presence of a new one. Remember, at this age memory is short. You may need to explain things to them over and over again.

Although these children have limited understanding, they can move easily between their parents' separate households if the moves are routine and explained to them in advance—and if they are allowed to take familiar items along with them, such as a blanket or stuffed animal. That may sound inconsequential to an adult, but it is very important to a child.

Elementary School Age: 6-12 Years. Children in this developmental level are the most apt to believe they were responsible for the divorce. And since they feel responsible for causing a break, they feel they should be able to bring their parents back together. Parents may hear such things as: "Daddy asked me about you today. He said I was pretty just like you, Mommy." or "I bet Mom still loves you. I can tell."

Let your child know he was in no way responsible for the divorce. Explain things to him in terms appropriate for his developmental level. Such questions as "Why did you get divorced?" and "Why did you marry someone else?" need to be answered without blaming or accusing your child, your ex-mate or yourself. Make sure you understand what your child is asking and only give the information he actually needs.

In this age group we also see the first appearance of grief in an adult-like sadness. Other symptomatic responses may include fear of abandonment, fear of the future and feelings of powerlessness.

Shortly after Adrienne and I were married, Nichole, then nine years old, dreamed several times that we died in an accident. Those dreams were not hidden wishes, but representations of her fear of being abandoned.

Children frequently hear their parents arguing prior to a divorce. They can feel their parents' animosity toward one another, and will often ask their parents if they are going to divorce. Too often parents deny the possibility because they don't want to worry the children or face the possibility themselves. Then when the divorce does come, the children may be left with two feelings: "People have no control over their lives," and "You can't trust your parents." They need to realize that divorce didn't just jump out and grab their parents; there are consequences for certain behaviors and actions.

Being plunged into the experience of their parents' divorce may give children the feeling they have no control over their lives. It helps children overcome their feelings of powerlessness if they are allowed to make minor decisions. They can choose between a hot lunch or a cold lunch, wearing a blue shirt or a brown shirt, doing homework the hour before supper or the hour after supper. The decisions should be appropriate for the child's age.

You can further help establish a child's sense of security by keeping your word. When you make a promise about anything—from a day in the park to consequences for misbehavior—keep it. This helps your child build trust in you. Later, when you say to him, "I'll be there when you need me," he will believe it.

Adolescents. A close friend of ours, who is also in the field of psychology, used to wonder how he would ever be able to let go of his children. The thought of turning them out into the cold, cruel world on their own was almost too much for him. Then he discovered that God does a wonderful thing for parents who are holding on to children too tightly. He turns them into adolescents.

How do you know when a child is a victim of adolescence? He complains all morning that he is too sick to go to school and warns he may die before second period. Then he breezes into the house after school shouting, "Where's my sweatsuit? I have to get ready for the basketball game tonight."

An adolescent will come home in tears, slam doors, gorge herself on ice cream, then spend three hours on the phone with her best friend working out a problem she told her mother didn't exist. Adolescents want your help. When you give it to them, they get furious.

All the dependent/independent conflicts a teenager normally goes through are intensified when their parents remarry. Lisa, one of my adolescent clients, described it to me this way:

"There's only one thing worse than living through your parents' divorce, and that's living through your mother's second marriage. There were a lot of things I didn't like when Mom was the only parent at home. I watched my brother and sisters after school until Mom got home from work. I had to cook and clean and do laundry. I had a lot of responsibilities, but Mom started treating me like an adult. I felt like we had become best friends. Now that she's married to Bob, she treats me like a kid again. I have all kinds of restrictions I didn't have before she remarried."

Like every adolescent, Lisa was striving to become more and more independent. When her mother remarried, Lisa felt like she had been demoted from Mother's best friend to Mother's child again. Her mother explained her actions by saying, "After I was divorced, I didn't have the time to be a good parent. Now I do and I'm going to be a good one."

The conflict for Lisa and her mother came in their separate goals. While her mother was trying to build a strong family unit in her second marriage, Lisa was working on establishing herself as an individual, not a family member. This is a common conflict even in the most solid of nuclear families. And it is a healthy conflict for the teen as long as it heads in positive directions. The key is to give adolescents the opportunity to experience independence through competence rather than through rebellion.

Adolescents often look to their peers for support. When their family life is going through stressful changes, they may seek out peer support even more. The older adolescent in a blended family may leave home more quickly than he would in a nuclear family for several reasons. Some are:

An uncaring or unloving stepparent

The biological parent's new-found strength to exercise authority, which places the adolescent back into the role of child

Feelings of neglect because of the biological parent's new mate

Unwillingness on the adolescent's part to develop new relationships within the blended family

Resentment over expectations to care for younger siblings or stepsiblings

Personally, I am very thankful Adrienne and I had several years of marriage and blended family life under our belts before Nichole hit her mid-teens. There have been times when I have taken her actions to mean rejection of me as the head of our household until I remind myself that it is not a question of parental rejection, but one of an adolescent's striving for independence.

Like Nichole, blended family adolescents face the double complications of finding independence in two households—their custodial home and their non-custodial home. Some teens have their efforts further thwarted because their parents send them back and forth between households on a supposedly "permanent" basis.

For example, Johnny tries to establish his independence (whether effectively or ineffectively) in his custodial household. If the stress level becomes too high, he is moved into his other household, where he still must establish his independence. If the pressure there becomes too great, he is sent back to his first household. Both households move him back and forth on a string of dependency like a yo-yo. The question shouldn't be where Johnny can live under the least amount of pressure. The issue is how best to help Johnny reach responsible independence.

Knowing they have someone to talk to is important for children of all ages and stages, but there are times children cannot talk to their parents. Rather than be hurt at what looks like rejection, parents can best help by encouraging their children to talk with others, whether friends or paid professionals. The more insight they gain and the more they are able to express their feelings, the more they will be able to complete the process of mourning for the loss of their nuclear family system.

Life in Two Households

As important as it is to address children's reactions to divorce and remarriage, the problems don't stop there. A big question parents should keep in mind is "How are my children reacting *today?*" More specifically, "How are they coping with living in two households?" and "How do they react to the way their biological parents act toward one another?"

Although I'm not a runner, I was one of the best fans our track team had, especially when it came to relay races. I loved to watch the individual styles of the runners. Rodney, the starter, moved like the classic short distance runner—light and swift. The second runner, Steve, was one of the biggest guys in our class. He ran like a workhorse, pounding and thundering down the track. Mike, the third man in the race, ran like a leaping deer, barely skimming the track. His stride was in direct contrast to that of the anchor man.

Greg's short, fast strides spun cinders like a dragster's tires. All four runners were unique in their running form, yet they all had the same goal—to get the baton across the finish line.

The runners in a blended family relay race may include the children's biological parents, stepparents and grandparents. The children are the batons and the finish line is emotional, spiritual and physical maturity for each child. The runners' attitudes, their willingness to share in a mutual goal and the way they exchange the baton are of critical importance.

In working with blended families we have seen several different "runner" attitudes. For instance:

The Star Runner. Star's attitude is, "I don't need the other runners to win this race." Star always has a reason for being unwilling to share the children:

> He (or she) left me and the kids. He can't possibly care about them.
>
> I left him because he's a bum. My children are better off without him.
>
> The children's other household is too lenient.
>
> The children's other household is too strict.
>
> The children's other biological parent isn't a Christian.
>
> They're nothing but a bunch of religious fanatics over there.

Some of these may be true, but the Star Runner needs to realize this is a relay race, not an individual event. The others may not run as well, but they must participate.

The Polly Gripper. You know Polly. The children have their hats, coats and mittens on, suitcases in hand, ready to walk out the door when she begins a twenty-minute discourse per child on how much she loves them, how much she will miss them and how lonely she will be without them all weekend. In the last picture the children have of Polly before going to Dad's house, she is standing outside without her coat in sub-zero weather, waving goodby with tears frozen to her cheeks.

Polly must remember that holding on to the baton is not the best way to get it to the finish line. Her high level of anxiety only creates anxiety in the children and prevents them from freely enjoying themselves, growing and learning in their other household. They may act out this anxiety by being fretful and worried, since they are wondering if Mom will be O.K. until they get back.

Polly's insistence on holding on to the baton even after placing it into the hand of the next runner in the other household could cause everyone to stumble—and it's painful for Polly. No one likes being dragged through the cinders. But Polly is deceived. Thinking her children are sharing her pain of separation, she tightens her grip all the more.

The Deliberately Hesitant Runner. Deliberately Hesitant is so afraid of getting entangled with the next runner that he tosses the baton instead of firmly placing it in his hand. Thus, he drops the children off an hour early at the local restaurant to wait for their other biological parent to pick them up. The exchange is usually confusing because all communication concerning pick-up time and length of stay is done through the children, not the parents!

Deliberately Hesitant should not see the next runner as his ex-mate, but as the children's other parent. The hand-off should always be sure, even if it means brief communication with the other runners.

The Gapper. This runner leaves a gap in the relay team. He is the one who, while enjoying a leisurely Saturday afternoon boating trip with friends, is suddenly reminded he has children.

"How's the kids, Gapper?"

"The kids? The kids! Oh, no! I was supposed to pick them up at nine this morning!"

Gapper's children were ready at eight o'clock, anxiously awaiting his arrival. At nine they were watching the driveway, knowing he would be there any minute. At ten they were trying to call him, but no one was home. At eleven they were bickering with each other, unwilling to admit Gapper had failed to show up again. At noon they were hungry but wouldn't eat, because Gapper had promised to take them to Hungry Tummy for lunch. They turned down invitations from friends to play because they just knew this time Gapper would be there.

At eight that evening their phone rings. "Hey, kids, I'm really sorry. I just got so busy today. You know how it is. It's really too late to come and get you now, but I'll see you next weekend, O.K.?"

It's not O.K. Gapper should be there to see how his failure to be involved in the race affects the whole team. The other runners were at their posts and the batons were more than ready for the exchange. Chronic gaps will ultimately affect his children's emotional health.

The Ruthless Runner. The second runner is ready for the hand-off. He realizes the importance of grabbing the baton securely. When the right time comes, he lunges ahead with his eyes fixed on the finish line, his open hand extended behind him ready to receive the baton. When the baton hits his hand he grips it, and immediately flinches in pain. Staring at the baton, he finds it covered with thorns. What relay runner would deliberately make the baton painful for the next runner? Ruthless.

In the time Ruthless has held the baton, she (or he) has filled it with cutting barbs. "I bet it's like a prison at your dad's house. His new stepchildren get everything they want, don't they, while we have to suffer because of it. While we're waiting on your dad and stepmother, why don't we read a story? How about Cinderella?"

One man shared with us how he was cut to shreds by his stepson's biological father during weekend visits: "Your stepdad is a real wimp and not a man. He has no right to discipline you. If he lays a hand on you or does anything you don't like, tell me and I'll beat him up."

Another man shared with us how the children's biological mother made up sordid details about him and their stepmother.

When the children return from a stay with Ruthless, it is no wonder they act strangely toward their custodial parent or stepparent. How would you feel about living with Cinderella's wicked stepmother? One of the saddest things about dealing with Ruthless is the other biological parent's hesitancy to accept the hand-off because it is so painful.

Although Ruthless may feel she has every right to lambaste her children's other household, she needs to realize that, in the long run, it is the children who are hurt the most. They need to be a part of their other household. When children are manipulated into defiance, that defiance can move against other authority figure relationships as well and can even backfire on Ruthless.

The Ideal Runner. The Ideal Runner is consistent and diligent with the foremost goal of getting the baton to the finish line. He is willing to put in the extra effort needed if another runner falls or isn't running up to capacity. And he keeps on going even when given a bad hand-off.

The Transition

Although some children look forward to staying in their other household on weekends, there are those children who arrive on Friday afternoon with an "I'm not going to be happy here, even if it kills me" attitude. Take Jimmy, for example.

"Jimmy, we're so glad you're here. Kari and I have really been looking forward to having you stay with us this weekend."

No response from Jimmy, who is sitting on the couch with his coat still on.

"Well," Dad says cheerfully. "We thought we'd take you out for a pizza. How does that sound?"

"Boring."

"Since when is pizza boring?"

"I like hamburger and french fries better."

"No problem. Hamburger and fries it is."

"But I'm not hungry for a hamburger tonight."

"Oh. What *would* you like to eat?"

Jimmy shrugs his shoulders.

"Kari, why don't we take Jimmy to that new video game and fast food place down on Franklin Street? What do you think, Jimmy?"

"I've already been there."

"Come on, Jimmy. We've got to eat somewhere. They serve tacos. Now I know you like tacos."

"Yeah. That's what I had for supper before I came."

And on it goes.

When I first began leading youth programs I was naive enough to walk in and ask, "What do you want to do first? Do you want to sing first?"

"Nah."

"Do you want to play a game first?"

"Nah."

"What do you want to do?"

"I don't know."

It didn't take long for me to realize the youths weren't going to make up a program that would make them happy. They told their parents it would be a drag and they had to be miserable to prove it.

Jimmy had already decided he was not going to enjoy himself at his dad's. He, like the youths on opening night at my retreats, was determined to have a terrible weekend. He was not going to accept any of his dad's suggestions or offer any ideas of his own. Rather than asking Jimmy to be enthusiastic before the program began, Dad needed to start the program and put Jimmy right in the middle of it.

Experience has taught me to create a high-energy Friday evening in my youth retreats or seminars, with lots of singing and activities. As the leader, it is my responsibility to establish the emotional climate and get the youths out of their cliques and into the program. What I want them to feel from me is, "I'm really looking forward to the great time we are going to have. I have a program and we're going to stick with it. If you join with me, we'll have a good time."

Blended families can follow this same strategy.

On the first evening when your non-custodial children come to stay for the weekend, you need to break down the barriers and become a family. Don't walk in, take their coats and plop down in front of the TV. This is family time. Be exciting. Play games. Be structured. Your children are keyed up over their visit. Put that energy into family building rather than leaving it as free-floating anxiety.

Be sensitive, though, to your children's personalities. A "three-ring circus" could make a quiet child uncomfortable. Find the balance.

There always came a time during the youth retreats to get down to business. After a rousing, fun-packed Friday evening, Saturday was a day for teaching and activities. In much the same way, it should not be all games when your non-custodial children stay for the week or weekend. You have to get on with the business of living, which means doing such things as: getting up at the regular time, eating well-balanced meals, doing chores, watching or not watching certain television programs, getting to bed at a reasonable hour, making it to church on Sunday morning.

Consistency is important for children in both households. This consistency should not only be within each separate household, but between households. If Johnny goes to bed at nine o'clock in his custodial household, his non-custodial household should aim for the same bedtime.

One stepmother shared with us how much she dreaded her stepchildren's visits. They came only one weekend a month, but once they were there they took command of the house. "They get into everything, do anything they want and eat everything in sight. The three of them go through a twelve-pack of ice cream bars within two hours. My kids come running to me saying, 'Mom, they just ate their fourth ice cream bar!' To which I say, 'It's O.K. Forget it.' To Frank I say, 'Frank, they just ate that whole package of ice cream bars I bought this morning.' And what does Frank say? 'Buy more ice cream bars.'"

Poor household structure only allows children to develop insolent attitudes. "Gee, we couldn't get away with this at home. Something must be wrong here." Plus, they may start to wonder what else they can get away with.

Consistency in expectations for the children is important for their adjustment within each household and between households. When your non-custodial children come to stay, let them know they are equal with the other children living in your household. They are no more or no less important. Everyone has the same privileges and shares in the responsibilities.

Remember, non-custodial children need their "space" and "stuff." Make sleeping arrangements prior to their arrival. Have some personal belongings at the house for them: toothbrush, extra pair of pajamas or nightgown, tennis shoes, jeans, a sweater or jacket and one dressy outfit. If your non-custodial children unexpectedly end up spending the night, they have their pajamas. If you plan on taking them out in style and they didn't bring an appropriate outfit, you can still dress them up.

Don't store their things in a brown paper bag and then dig it out of the closet in front of them. Find a permanent spot and make it easily accessible for the children.

One mother shared with us how her daughters' stepmother has a room just for them. She keeps pictures of the girls up, leaves items out that the girls have made and sends them letters and pictures to keep them up-to-date on what is happening in their other household.

If you have custodial children the same age as your non-custodial children, forming friendships with neighborhood children will probably come naturally. If not, you may need to step in and help them by getting to know your neighbors and finding children around the same age for them to play with during their stay.

Leaving Home to Go Home

Why is it, after a beautiful weekend, little Harold and Susie begin to act obnoxious, and you wonder, "Why in the world is this happening! We've had a wonderful weekend."

The reason may not be reasonable. The children may be thinking, "It's easier for me to leave if Dad and Stepmom are mad at me." This approach is less painful for some children than crying, hugging and feeling sad when they have to leave. If you are angry with them, they can be angry with you. If they are angry with you, they don't have to think about how much it hurts to leave or how much they will miss you.

As the custodial parent, you may notice your children acting differently when they arrive home from their other household. Your children's two separate households can only be in sync up to a point, especially if there are hard feelings between biological parents. Even though the rules may be similar, the personalities are different.

During the time your children are out of your household they are marching to a different beat. That doesn't mean the other household has a bad system, just one that's different from yours. It takes time to get back in rhythm with the old beat. Be aware of your children's need for time to make the transition.

Rivalry Between Stepchildren

Fighting between siblings occurs in every family, nuclear or blended. Children fight for position, power, the television, the best piece of meat, the last french fry, the first french fry, the bathroom, the top bunk and the bottom bunk. Children will always find something to argue about.

The important thing is for parents not to supply the ammunition.

Jim and Joann were on a family vacation with their two sets of children, neither of which lived with them. While in a souvenir shop, Jim purchased matching sweatshirts for his children without offering to buy anything for his stepchildren. All the way back to the motel, Joann's children seized every opportunity to harass Jim's children. By evening Jim's children jumped in and declared all-out war. Tired of their children's continual fighting and bickering, Jim and Joann enforced a truce.

After a short investigation, Joann discovered the ill feelings were caused by the sweatshirt purchases. When she asked her children, "Do you want us to go back in the morning and buy you each a sweatshirt?" they answered, "No." They didn't want sweatshirts, they wanted to be treated fairly and with consideration by Jim.

Step back and ask yourself these questions. "Do I treat my stepchildren the same as my own children? Am I doing for my children and undoing for my stepchildren? Am I giving my children and stepchildren reasons to fight?"

At this point, we are not talking about how you *feel* toward your children and stepchildren, but how you *act* toward them. It is unrealistic to think you can feel as strongly toward children you have lived with for a short time as you do for the children you have lived with since birth, but you can act the same toward them.

Even in nuclear families, parents often have one child they protect or defend more than others. This viewpoint is especially tragic in a blended family system when "your" child is always the instigator and "my" child is always the poor victim.

When a one-sided attitude develops, it may be because you or your mate listens to or hears only one side of the story. Strive to be united. The two of you can then piece together the information to make the best judgment in conflicts between stepsiblings.

In Chapter 3 we discussed the issue of fairness between children and the need to have the same behavior expectations for both your children and stepchildren. This fairness is important not only to strengthen the relationship between mates, but also to reduce rivalry between stepsiblings. Fitting your non-custodial children into the regular pattern of your household (i.e., chores, basic rules and responsibilities) helps both your custodial and non-custodial children feel they are on more equal ground

Loyalty Conflicts

What is a loyalty conflict? Jesus addressed this question when talking with the Pharisees about paying taxes to Caesar: "Give to Caesar what is Caesar's, and to God what is God's" (Matthew 22:21).

When applied to loyalty conflicts in blended families, the above passage might read, "Give to your biological parent what belongs to your biological parent, and to your stepparent what belongs to your stepparent."

If Benny is receiving love, nurturing and emotional support from his stepparents, then he should be able to return those things to his stepparents without feeling he is robbing his biological parents. And stepparents should recognize that Benny's need to share those things with his biological parents does not mean that the stepparent relationship is of little importance.

Loyalty conflicts can be deflated or inflated based on our reactions when our children express praise for the parents in their other household. If we respond with snide remarks, the children are torn by thinking they don't have our permission to love the other important people in their lives.

Loyalty conflicts are not always between a biological parent and stepparent. One or both biological parents can cause a child to have loyalty conflicts.

Glen's children were between the ages of eight and thirteen when he went through a trying divorce. Over the next few years the animosity of his ex-mate, Darlene, who had custody of the children, made relating with his children difficult, particularly with his oldest daughter, Marsha.

Marsha's mother insisted the children not tell their father anything about their custodial household. "If you tell him anything, he will take you away from me and I'll be left all alone."

One afternoon when Glen called Darlene to make arrangements to pick up his children for the weekend, Darlene's mother picked up the phone and took the opportunity to tell Glen what a bum he was. He could hear Marsha in the background saying, "You tell him, Grandma."

Darlene's propaganda had worked. Marsha had chosen sides. From that point on she refused to see Glen and spoke badly of him to her brothers. Within a few months her mother remarried and Marsha took her new stepfather's last name.

For two long years after that Glen tried to keep in touch with Marsha. He sent Christmas presents, cards and letters, but heard nothing.

During that time, however, Marsha was beginning to think for herself. She watched as her mother's second marriage crumbled and decided she had been wrong about her father. Two weeks after her eighteenth birthday, she called Glen and they were able to renew their relationship. It is sad to think that they lost five years of relating because one parent pushed the loyalty conflict to the limit.

Granting your children permission to love their other parent and stepparent will better equip them for a healthy emotional life. A parent's role is to help his children resolve their conflicts, not add to them.

Sexuality in Blended Families

Sexuality is a much greater issue in blended families than in nuclear families. In blended families there is a greater awareness of sexuality, a greater potential for sexual contact between children in the household and a greater possibility for sexual contact between the stepparent and stepchild.

In early adolescence, children in nuclear families rarely think of their parents as sexual beings. But when a twelve- or thirteen-year-old child's parent remarries and runs off on a honeymoon, the child stops in his tracks and says, "Wait a minute. Honeymoons are for hugging and kissing and romance. Are they doing that? My mom with that man?" or "My dad with that woman?"

When parents in a nuclear family have a high level of passion toward one another in their first years of marriage, the children either have not arrived yet or are toddlers. When all that electricity flowed between the two of them, the children had no idea what electricity was. Then, when the children were older, the parents had the electric flow under control. This is not the case in a second marriage. When the passion starts to flow, adolescent children can figure out what's going on.

Incestuous relationships in both nuclear and blended families in the United States are a growing problem. You may need to address this problem as an issue in your home and recognize it as a potential threat to your family life.

One of the most foolish actions on the part of parents I have ever heard in my office was told me by a young woman who was thirteen at the time her mother remarried: "When my mom and stepdad were married, there weren't enough bedrooms or beds; so I slept in the same bed as my fifteen-year-old stepbrother." They began having intercourse almost immediately. The sleeping arrangements were eventually changed, but her stepbrother continued to visit her bedroom at night for several months.

Whatever were the parents thinking? Were they thinking at all? Even in a nuclear family, such sleeping arrangements should be unheard of.

A few safeguards in blended family living can help reduce sexually tempting situations. Parents may need to tone down their displays of affection, for instance, in their children's presence. Living arrangements need to be worked out for privacy. Make sure family members are not walking in on each other while changing clothes or bathing. And clear limits on appropriate dress around the house must be established. Neither girls nor boys should be allowed to run around in their underwear.

If your teenaged stepdaughter spends the whole evening in her baby doll pajamas, let your wife know you find it inappropriate. "Hey listen, honey, I don't want to sound depraved, but it bothers me when Sharon spends all evening with the family in those skimpy pajamas. Would you please ask her to wear a robe or something less revealing?" If your stepson wants to stay cool by just wearing his underwear and it bothers you, ask Dad to tell him to wear his shorts. They may have always worn revealing clothes around the house, but this is a new home and a new family situation.

If your children are going to react to sexual issues, you want them reacting in normal healthy ways. You can help them do this by requiring appropriate dress and actions and by keeping private what should be kept private.

Belonging

Abraham Maslow developed a list on the hierarchy of the five basic human needs. They are:

Physical: food and water
Security: shelter
Belonging: a sense of being loved
Purpose: a reason for being
Self-actualization: the desire to realize one's fullest
        potential

Some parents and stepparents feel their job is finished once they have provided their children with the first two basic needs: something to eat and a place to live. They feel it is up to the children to do the rest. But for the child whose emotions are already torn between two households, the third need, a message of "you belong," is vitally important. If it is not clear, a child may camouflage the desire to know he belongs by misbehavior or overt competition. His level of insecurity may grow to the point where he will compete with everyone in the household for his biological parent's time and affection.

Stepparents should never openly compete with their stepchildren for the biological parent's attentions. I have seen blended families in which the stepparents would not stop trying to compete and, in each case, the home situation was disastrous. Stepparents need to work on providing love and a sense of belonging for the children, not trying to take away the security they need from their biological parents.

A child's need for a sense of belonging intensifies around the holidays as his thoughts turn to the absence of his non-custodial parent and his other household's extended family. Expressing love for him and making him a part of holiday planning will help him through the difficulties of extended holiday visits. Pre-planning sparks a child's anticipation of holiday activities. And when he anticipates something good happening, he is not as preoccupied with worry over what he wishes would happen.

The most meaningful aspect shaping young people's lives is their daily interaction with "significant others"— Mom, Dad, Stepmom, Stepdad, siblings and stepsiblings. How they see those in close relationship with themselves interacting with one another is also important. Your children's ability to move confidently between households will be based largely on the quality of those relationships.

5

Stepping In As a Stepparent

When you marry and form a nuclear family, you usually have one set of in-laws and one set of children. Marrying into a blended family, however, is like jumping head first into chaos.

You can imagine some of the tangled conversations: "A fishing trip Saturday sounds great, Bruce. But wait. I can't seem to remember if we had my kids two weekends ago or three. If it was two, we'll be there. If it was three, my kids will be here and I'd just as soon not be away. But then again, we'd have to get a sitter for Tom and Don anyway—that is, if they don't go to their dad's this weekend."

The possible number of family combinations and relationships in blended families can be mind-boggling. Both parents may or may not have custody of children and may have children of their own. If the father or mother has children from two previous marriages the combinations become even more complex.

As if keeping the logistics straight isn't enough, there are times a stepparent feels he just can't win. He works hard at being Mr. Wonderful for the kids who respond by murmuring, "Get out of my life." While defending his wife from her teenage son, she turns to him and says, "If you don't mind, this is a family matter." His lawyer calls to say that his wife's ex-husband is taking her to court again over visitation. The week before, his ex-wife threw everything he ever gave their children out on the front lawn and shouted, "Nothing you give these kids will ever make up for what you've done to them!" His parents still aren't talking to him because they think he married into a family with more problems than he can handle. And he is beginning to wonder if they are right.

One stepfather told me he announced to his stepchildren over the din of depressing circumstances, "I am going to love your mother. I may not know anything else, but I know I am going to love your mother." He had no idea what was happening in his blended family or how to control it, but he knew somehow his love for his wife was the first step in putting things in order.

Although he had taken a good first step by committing himself to his relationship with his wife, this stepparent needed to know what the next steps were. By understanding what was happening in his blended family and why, he and his wife could sort out the confusion and repeated hassles together.

The next three sections—Stepping In from the Outside, Stepping Into a New Role, and Stepping Into New and Different Relationships—will help both the stepparent and biological parent understand what transpires when the husband, wife or both step in as a stepparent.

Stepping In from the Outside

When I married Adrienne I was the newcomer stepping in from the outside, both physically and experientially.

Physically, I moved into their home. Experientially, I moved into their whole family system.

While we had dated, I was the visitor, the one who occasionally mowed her yard, hammered a loose nail, turned on the sprinkler and then went home. On the day we married I became a permanent resident at Adrienne's house. But mentally stepping out of my visitor role into my resident role, and feeling like her home was now my home, took a little longer. Initially, I still felt like a visitor coming to stay at "her" house. The tools I used to do work around the house had the girls' father's name on them, and I eased into the Lazy Boy in the family room thinking, *This is probably his chair, too.*

A friend of ours described the same feeling when he first remarried. "When I came home and Marge wasn't there, I felt I should sit in the living room and wait for her. It still seemed like her house, not ours."

The physical nature of the new home may not be the only reason for feeling like an outsider. The depth of the relationship between your new mate and his or her biological children can often leave you feeling excluded. It takes a long time to develop close relationships; no one can expect to experience the same level of intimacy the children have with their biological parent simply by moving into the house.

Naturally, in their years of living together your mate and his or her children have developed inside stories that you know nothing about. My not understanding Adrienne and the girls' inside jokes probably contributed the most to my feeling like a rookie on the team. They had words and little phrases that would send them into gales of laughter while I sat by.

The first Thanksgiving we spent together as a family, for example, one of the girls said, "Mom, remember the turkey?" They laughed hysterically until finally I asked, "What's so funny?" When they explained to me how Adrienne had broiled a turkey for three hours one Thanksgiving, I thought it was funny, but not that funny.

"Isn't that crazy, Dad?" they asked.

When I had no reply, they chimed in, "Well, you had to be there."

It is surprising how much family wit, jokes and humor can include or exclude newcomers. Rather than feeling like an outsider, your willingness to try and understand the inside jokes and patterns of humor and to laugh along will make stepping in from the outside much easier. Don't be afraid to say, "What does that mean?" or "I don't understand. Would you explain that to me?" They will enjoy sharing the story with you and you will be able to relax and feel included.

It has been said that 7 percent of communication is in the content of the words, 38 percent is in the tone of voice and 55 percent is in the body language. If 93 percent of communication is based on tone and body language, and you're new to the system, it is no wonder you think you are missing a lot. You are. If Tony giggles when he is being reprimanded, Mom knows it is only nervous laughter, while you may see it as a flagrant display of disrespect.

When you step into your blended family, you need to realize that it takes time to understand a communication system that has been growing and developing for years. Much of the communication going on between your mate and his children is far too subtle to be identified quickly. This subtlety is not a clever technique devised to keep you on the ouside, but the result of years of fine tuning.

One of your early tasks as you step in from the outside is to become aware of and try to learn the communication system already in progress. In time you will be a vital part of it.

Slowly but surely, Adrienne, the girls and I have collected memories that are meaningful to us as a family. The words *Incredible Hulk* put all of us into stitches but—well, you had to be there.

The Extended Family. One Saturday morning at the breakfast table the girls were talking about Uncle Bill. Wanting to be a part of their conversation, I asked casually, "Who's Uncle Bill?"

Adrienne, with her nose still in the morning paper, said, "Tom, Uncle Bill is your uncle. You know, the one married to Aunt Dorothy."

"Adrienne, I know who my Uncle Bill is. Nichole wasn't talking about my Uncle Bill."

Adrienne went on. "Oh, well. Then Uncle Bill is my uncle who is married to my mother's sister Louella. They live in Chicago."

"No, Mom," Nichole said. "We were talking about Uncle Bill and Robbie."

"Oh." Adrienne began again. "Tom, they weren't talking about my uncle; they meant Bill and Robbie."

With no further explanation, I began thinking out loud. "Robbie. That's a funny name for a woman. Aunt Robbie, huh?"

The girls burst into giggles.

"Dad, Robbie isn't our aunt. He's Uncle Bill's son!"

The girls continued eating until Jennifer half-asked, half-stated, "Nichole, isn't Aunt Suzanne funny?"

After contemplating whether or not I really wanted to go through that again, I asked, "Who's Aunt Suzanne?"

Adrienne surfaced again. "Aunt Suzanne is . . . is . . . I don't know any Aunt Suzanne! Girls, who is she?"

When I stepped into my blended family, I also stumbled into a whole new extended family system I knew very little about. Who *were* Uncle Bill, Robbie, Uncle David, Aunt

Iola, Cindy and Pat? Were they from Adrienne's side of the family or the girls' biological father's side of the family? There were even some names Adrienne knew nothing about and it dawned on us that there was another whole set of relatives we would never know, but who knew and interacted with our girls.

A more immediate problem than wondering who some of those people are, however, is getting along with the immediate family. "Will they compare me with the girls' father? Will they welcome me as an in-law?"

When visiting your in-laws, you can be sure that old home movies and photograph albums lurk somewhere in their houses. There may even be family portraits hanging on the wall that include your mate, your stepchildren, and the phantom "ex." Don't be surprised if, after an evening of viewing home movies, you dream of drawing black moustaches on the phantom.

Dreaming is one thing, but back in real life you can't edit out portions of a person's life, particularly when it involves your blended family. Even though they are old memories, they are a special part of each family member. Try not to be overly sensitive. Ask your mate to encourage his or her extended family to have your feelings in mind when they bring out the family photos.

One stepmother shared with us the hurt she felt every time she looked at the family photo wall at her mother-in-law's. There hung a family portrait of her husband, the children and his ex-wife.

One weekend, however, her brother-in-law took a snapshot of the new family, had it blown up and gave it to his mother to replace the "old" picture. She shared with us how overjoyed she was to see the picture on display, and how happy her mother-in-law was to have a recent picture of the family.

As the newcomer, you need to remember that the pictures and home movies of the family were collected from years of experiences and shared activities. In time there will be new family memories to share with your extended family. In the meantime, there are some steps you can take to help that process along.

If you don't have a good camera, buy one, and make sure you take it along on family outings. Then have two copies made of special family pictures. Offer copies to your mate's extended family and start a family photo album at home.

Being left out of jokes, having communication float right over your head and not having your picture on the wall may cause you to feel you are not accepted in your blended family. Stepping in as a stepparent is a process, not a one-time event. Remember, time is on your side.

Stepping Into a New Role

What an image we stepparents have to live down!

The very word stepmother brings to many people's minds the storybook image of a wicked, self-centered woman who dresses her children in diamonds and "his little urchins" in rags. Stepfathers, like David Copperfield's black-hearted Mr. Murdstone, are depicted as devious, merciless men who dress *everybody* in rags.

Stepparents can find themselves facing an identity crisis from the many roles they are expected to fill. One might well complain, "Sometimes my wife asks me to be a parent, meaning, jump right in and take the initiative. Sometimes I'm supposed to be a stepparent, meaning, check it out with her first, then take the initiative. And at other times I'm not supposed to be a parent at all, just a shadow in the background. Yet I'm supposed to love my stepchildren as if they were my own."

When you think about the roles of a parent, does the word step affect your definition? Do you consider the step-parent's role a step away from being a "real" parent? Or a step under what is required to be a parent? Do you feel the world's eyes on you, ready to judge? Or do you compare yourself to your mate's "ex"?

Rather than modeling your role as a stepparent after anyone else, why not base it on the unchanging attributes of the heavenly Father. He reveals the ultimate in parental attitudes, combining unmerited love (John 3:16, Ephesians 2:8-9), fairness (Acts 10:34, Romans 10:12), attentiveness (Luke 12:6-7, I Peter 5:7) and discipline (Hebrews 12:5).

Adrienne and I have put together a checklist of words that describe parental attitudes and characteristics. On a scale of one to five, rate with a checkmark how important you feel it is for a parent to be:

	Low 1	2	3	4	High 5
1. Available					
2. Affectionate					
3. Faithful					
4. Fair					
5. Patient					
6. Merciful					
7. Accepting					

8. Consistent					
9. Loving					
10. Encouraging					
11. Understanding					
12. Attentive					
13. A provider					
14. A leader					
15. A protector					
16. Trusting					
17. Enthusiastic					
18. Sincere					
19. Firm					
20. A disciplinarian					
21. An example					
22. Helpful					
23. A counselor					

24. A confidant					
25. Reasonable					
Endowed with a 26. sense of humor					

When you have finished checking the above list, go back and rate yourself by placing an *x* under the number you feel indicates the level at which you are fulfilling that description.

Now compare the *x*'s and checks. How much of a discrepancy is there between the ideal and the real?

Your role may be shaped by the needs presented in your household. Some children require more encouragement while others require more discipline. Some children may need to learn how to laugh and enjoy life while others may need an example of responsibility. What are the needs of your household? Do you and your mate agree on those needs? If you don't, can you come to an agreement?

Go back to the checklist and place the initial of each child in your blended family next to the adjectives he or she needs more of. Identify these areas as goals to work toward.

Remember, as a stepparent you are a parent in process. You are moving from the real to the ideal, accepting yourself as you are, but striving to improve. Remember, too, you have a perfect example of parenthood in the heavenly Father.

Stepping Into New and Different Responsibilities

There are some obvious responsibilites of parenting and some not so obvious ones.

Classed with the former are food, clothing, dentist's appointments, heat, lights and transportation. Not so obvious, but equally important, are developing the children's attitudes toward marriage, themselves, life in general and toward God.

Marriage. Children who have experienced the arguing, anger and hurt of divorce may have a dim view of marriage. They may see family life as broken and fragmented. Parents and stepparents need to teach a biblical perspective of marriage and family life by example.

Self-Worth. As part of my clinical interviews, I frequently ask a client if he or she had any nicknames at home. Debbie, a young woman in her early twenties, answered in the affirmative. "My nickname was Dummy. Dad called me Dummy for as long as I can remember." Throughout school, Debbie proved faithfully that her father was right.

When I began counseling Debbie, I gave her an I.Q. test. She scored in the ninety-fifth percentile, which meant Debbie had more intellectual capacity than ninety-five out of one hundred people. Debbie is no dummy. Yet she had accepted her father's attitude about her as being true.

My attitude toward the children in my blended family will affect their attitude toward themselves. In particular, it will affect their sense of personal value and competence. One of our goals as parents is helping them feel more confident about tackling life's problems.

Attitude Toward Life. When children feel good about themselves, they begin to realize circumstances do not have to control them. This is especially important for children of divorce. The self-defeating belief, "I'm this way because my mom and dad were divorced when I was young," is not a statement children need to continue validating as they go through life. They need to be taught that a person's background does not have to determine his or her present behavior. There is a choice.

The Heavenly Father. Many children picture God much the same as they picture their earthly father, whether biological, step, or both. If their earthly father is strict, then God is strict. If he is unforgiving, then God is unforgiving. If he is loving and merciful, then God is loving and merciful.

Todd was one of dozens of clients reared in homes with angry or absent fathers. "Intellectually, I know from studying the Bible that God is loving and forgiving. I have even experienced it personally. But on a gut level, I keep waiting for Him to be just like my father." Even though Todd had a conversion experience and felt the love of the heavenly Father in Jesus, he kept waiting for Him to show His true colors. He just knew God would eventually become angry and reject him. Todd's worry seldom allowed him to rest in God's caring, loving arms.

Although I know I will fall short, I want to present the loving, just, firm, attentive character of God the Father to the children in my blended family. And Adrienne's role as mother can either help or hinder my ability. If she overrides my decisions in front of the children, acknowledges my wishes verbally but does whatever she wishes, or blocks any discipline I try to administer, she is, in essence, saying, "When the chips are down, fathers really don't count." Then when our children consider obedience before God, they may think they can sneak by Him, ignore Him, or give Him lipservice but still do exactly as they please.

Especially for Mothers/Stepmothers

More often than not it is the mother/stepmother who sets the pace in the household. She is the one responsible for scheduling everything from laundry to her family's social life. If your family grew considerably when you remarried, you may be feeling the need to become better organized. This section has a few suggestions that might help.

The Communication Complex. Organize a Communication Complex near your kitchen phone. Hang a bulletin board on the wall with the following items attached:

> Thumb tacks or push pins.
>
> A pencil connected by string.
>
> Two notepads, one for messages, one for groceries.
>
> A list of emergency and frequently called numbers: i.e., police, fire, ambulance, poison control center, doctor, dentist, pastor, schools, grandparents, neighbors.
>
> An open envelope tacked to the bulletin board marked Errands. Have each family member write down errands they need to have run on slips of paper, including times and dates, and drop them into the errand envelope.
>
> A large yearly calendar. Keeping a family calendar will be a big help in organizing all your family's activities. By writing in upcoming events, even routine ones, everyone will know what the others are doing and be able to make plans accordingly. It can also settle arguments over who had the car last on Saturday night.

Organize Your Family Calendar. Make a list of everyone's routine activities, including those of the children in the other households who stay with you. For example:

Jennifer: Ballet lessons - Mondays 5:45-6:30

> Brownies   - Tuesdays 3:30-4:15
> Youth Club   - Thursdays 5:00-7:00
> Allergy shots - Fridays after school

Transfer the list to the family calendar on the bulletin board. Then add other activities such as doctor or dentist appointments and the annual church picnic. Work out conflicts in schedules, including who takes whom where and when.

Organize Your Household. Working out a weekly plan to run your household will help your blended family life run smoother. As a home executor, the weekly jobs you need to accomplish can be divided into the following main categories.

> Meal planning, preparation and clean-up
> Errands and grocery shopping
> Laundry, ironing and mending
> Paying bills, sorting and filing mail, and
>   answering correspondence
> Cleaning

These main household jobs can be organized into specific days of the week. The children's chores, such as setting and clearing the table, should also be clearly defined.

If you also work outside your home, organize your household jobs around a morning, evening and Saturday schedule, splitting them up to fit your work timetable and your energy peaks.

Spontaneous Hassles. Spontaneous hassles are the "instant panic" episodes in your life. They are the times when your family expects you to drop whatever you are doing and come through in a flash like Wonder Woman. Hearing Cassandra yell, "I need six dozen cookies for Brownies after school," as she flies out the front door to catch the bus is a spontaneous hassle. The "short-order breakfast cook" faces another. Cassandra will eat cereal. Eric hates eggs and French toast, but might eat bacon and English muffins. Sandy will eat nothing but toasted cheese or leftover spaghetti. And Brett won't eat anything.

Your household plan for the week will let everyone know when you run errands, wash clothes, grocery shop and bake. After a two-month grace period, your family should be expected to conform to the plan.

If Cassandra has known for two weeks she needed six dozen cookies for Brownies and tells you at the last minute, don't spend all morning baking cookies. Give her a choice. "Either I buy the cookies with money out of your allowance or you don't take cookies to Brownies."

To eliminate the scramble over breakfast foods, make a menu for the week. Plan to prepare something each one likes at least once. Let your family know you are not a short-order cook and you are going to cook only what is on the menu.

Many of the spontaneous hassles you experience are really your children's hassles. A true super-hero is the woman who resists the temptation to spin around and miraculously produce six dozen cookies and a smorgasbord for breakfast in record time. Let the children experience the consequences of their actions. You will have fewer "instant panics" and more responsible children.

There are several reasons why it might be more difficult for you to put a household schedule into operation as a stepmother than as a mother in a nuclear family.

Perhaps you have gone from a simple, quiet lifestyle to a very confusing one with stepchildren bouncing off the walls. You may be completely overwhelmed and find it difficult to organize so many people.

Maybe you don't have the support you need from the

children's father. If that were the case with Cassandra, Dad may have yelled from the bathroom, "Hey, come on! You're just being mean to my kid. Make the cookies for her." A stepparent and biological parent need to be unified in all family concerns, including the household schedule.

You may be afraid of being too strict with your step-children and too lenient with your biological children.

Or you may not have the courage to enforce the household schedule with your stepchildren for fear they won't like you.

Managing your time and establishing order may not be easy, especially if you are not an organizer by nature. But you will find that it is acutally much easier to be fair to both your biological children and stepchildren when you have a household plan than when everything is up for grabs. Don't worry about losing your stepchildren's love. More likely than not, they will appreciate knowing what they can and cannot expect from you.

You and Your Mate

The busier your schedule, the less likely you are to have time alone with your mate. Yet this is very important. The two of you need to be alone together. There are a couple of things you can do to make that time.

Stress bedtime for younger children (8:00 or 8:30) and one or two nights a week ask the adolescent children in your home to head for their rooms around 9:00 to wind down from the day. They can read, listen to music or even go to sleep, but let them know that on those evenings from 9:00 on is your time to be together.

Continue to date your mate. Your date need not include a corsage and Master Charge, but it should include privacy and romance. You may enjoy a quiet time together over coffee and dessert in a favorite little restaurant. Although inexpensive, this kind of date can be one of the best for relationship building; it lets you focus in on one another and what is happening in your lives. A dinner date or a weekend getaway every couple of months is a great idea if it is financially feasible.

Don't become so caught up in your children, work or activities outside the home that you haven't time for one another. Remember, your love relationship with your mate sets the tone for the home. Don't feel guilty about taking the time to make it solid.

Working Through Finances

As we pointed out in an earlier chapter, financial pressures are the second major cause of divorce in remarriages. Listed below are some of the more frequent statements we have heard from husbands and wives involving finances in blended families.

"My husband pays child support to his ex, leaving less money for us."

"I pay child support every month, but I have no control over how it is spent on the kids. I don't even know if it is."

"The support money I receive for my children should not go into paying bills or the monthly budget. It belongs solely to my children."

"Our monthly budget is two hundred dollars more than our monthly income."

"He makes me feel guilty every time I want to buy something special for my children."

"I didn't mind giving money to my stepchildren at first, but they never appreciate it."

"My money is my money and her money is her money. I've been cleaned out once, and I'm not about to let it happen again."

"I had to go to work to pay off the charge accounts his ex ran up before their divorce was final."

"We might possibly get ahead financially, if her ex would quit taking us back to court."

Every blended family has different financial problems and needs. Although we can't give you a clear-cut financial plan, Adrienne and I would like to share some points we have found to be of importance to us.

We plan on our marriage lasting and handle our money with that in mind. We put all of our money into one pot: What is mine is Adrienne's and what is hers is mine. And it all belongs to the Lord.

We own everything jointly (the car, the house) and we usually discuss every expenditure, even at the ten- or twenty-dollar range.

We are both responsible for the financial well-being of our blended family. I work to make a living and Adrienne spends the money wisely—shopping for bargains and planning affordable meals.

We further try to eliminate waste by teaching our children good principles: turning off lights when no one is in the room and making sure doors are shut tightly during the winter when the heat is on. We teach them respect for personal and family property: hanging up their clothes and opening the car doors carefully in the garage.

The two of you should sit down and discuss your financial obligations and responsibilities, then develop a budget and follow it. Find the financial plan that works best for you. If necessary, consult a financial adviser.

Stepping Up

A stepparent's job takes adjusting, dedication and work. Here are eight steps to help you build better relationships.

Step One: Accept the fact that you are a stepparent in a blended family. It will never be a nuclear family. You will have to deal with ex-mates, visitation and a variety of issues. Even though your situation may place limitations on certain aspects of your family life, it does not have to restrict your family relationships. You can learn to care for, respect and trust each other.

Step Two: Educate yourself. Parenting is not an inborn skill. If parents in nuclear families should study up on parenting, how much more should blended family parents! Read about stepparenting and if possible attend group experiences with other stepparents. Ask questions; there is no better way to learn. Parents and stepparents frequently share with us what a relief it is to find that their experiences are not unique; other people are going through the same thing. If possible you may want to organize a group in your church to share, support and learn from one another.

Step Three: Work toward understanding. Never assume you completely understand what your mate, your children or your stepchildren are saying or feeling. Ask questions and listen carefully.

Step Four: Be definite in your objectives. Refer to the checklist you completed earlier in this chapter. Having identified the needs of your children, set specific objectives for yourself to meet those needs.

Step Five: Be structured, yet flexible. Children thrive on structure. It gives them a sense of security and offers boundaries wherein they can safely operate. But remember, people grow and circumstances change, making flexibility a must.

Step Six: Learn how to market yourself. Think of yourself as a product that you are "selling" to your blended family. If your price is too high (you are too demanding) no one will buy the product. If your price is too low (you don't ask for respect) the product may be seen as having little value.

Step Seven: Exercise forgiveness. Your ability to do this is crucial. It can tear down roadblocks that may be preventing the formation of quality relationships.

Step Eight: Learn to laugh. Laughter is a healing balm. Make sure there is plenty of it in your home. Laugh with your family. Laugh at yourself. Laugh at your mistakes and press on.

6

Bonding

From the moment Luke was born I thought he was the most beautiful baby I had ever seen. When the doctor lifted him from his mother's arms and handed him to me, Luke looked straight at me with his eyes wide open, and I loved him. As I studied his tiny features happily I thought about our earlier questions of bringing another child to our blended family.

The idea came up one October weekend when Adrienne and I babysat for a sweet-spirited, blue-eyed baby named Joshua. He slept in a wooden cradle at the foot of our bed and greeted us early in the morning with a smile. The girls were captivated by him. We all were.

All it took was my casual comment about enjoying having a baby around for Adrienne to talk me into placing an order. After a couple of weeks, though, we struggled with the pros and cons and decided it probably wasn't such a good idea. It would mean many adjustments for the entire family. One month later we found out our order was being filled anyway.

We pored over books that told us how the baby was

progressing, and when we learned in Adrienne's sixth month that his hearing was developed, we all began talking to Adrienne's tummy. In the evenings I would conclude my prayers by putting my mouth close to Adrienne's stomach and singing "Jesus Loves Me." Adrienne thought it was cute—a little strange, but cute.

Then, that day in the birthing room as I held Luke in my arms, I began singing "Jesus Loves Me" to him as I had so many times before. He watched me intently, trying to focus in on the face that belonged to the voice he already knew. I knew in that moment that something very special was happening.

Luke and I were bonding.

After having gone through the birth experience with Luke, I began to wish I could have done the same with Nichole and Jennifer. That, of course, was impossible. Step-parents cannot turn back the clock and be present at the births of their stepchildren. And a bonding, or uniting, relationship is not guaranteed as part of the blended family package. But we can find ways for bonding to take place.

As I investigate family relationships, I find people using the same three basic skills I use in counseling: acceptance, empathy and genuineness. Most parents use them unknowingly. Here's how they work.

Acceptance

Along with my private practice, I have worked with hundreds of students while consulting in public schools. When a teenager is given the ultimatum of either talking with me or taking a three-day suspension I know he is not coming to me eagerly, or by choice. As a consulting counselor, it is my first job to develop a good relationship with him. In his eyes

I have to go from being "the shrink" to a trusted friend, and in my eyes he has to go from being a "rotten kid" to a unique person. He may slouch down in his chair and tell me all the rotten things he has ever done but I don't grab him by the collar and scream in his face that he is a terrible kid.

At the same time I don't laugh with him over his bad behavior. I let him know that there are times when we all do things we are later ashamed of or recognize as wrong. I explain that we can figure out what makes him tick, and that I believe he is capable of changing some of the bad behavior that gets him into trouble.

This kind of acceptance is the foundation of a deepening relationship. All of us will do things we wish we hadn't, and not do things we wish we had. But just as we accept ourselves, we need to accept our stepchildren and at the same time believe they are capable of growth. And to foster growth, we need not to condemn or accuse, but to challenge, motivate and trust.

A friend of ours took that approach with his stepdaughter, Dawn, who was not doing well in school. Jack told her, "I know you're smart enough to get better grades. Let's see what would happen if you studied an hour every night from now until report card time. You may surprise yourself."

Together they worked to find the best time for her to study every night. For the entire nine weeks of that grading period, Jack encouraged her with positive comments.

At last one day the phone rang at his office. It was Dawn, calling from home, report card in hand, brimming with eagerness to tell the good news about her grades. They shared in her success together; Jack's trust in her ability gave Dawn the motivation she needed. Trust, one of the

trust

elements of acceptance, says, "I believe in you. You have integrity. I will place confidence in you."

Integrity, in turn, implies that a person can and will do what he says he will do. The older a person becomes and the better he knows himself, the more integrity he can have. It is not uncommon for a child or adolescent to think he can do something that is beyond his ability.

Suppose Dawn convinced Jack she could bring home all A's on her next report card. If she did the best she could do and her marks included a few B's and C's, that would not mean she had been untrustworthy in her study habits and broken her word. It would simply mean that there was a difference between what she thought she could do and what she was capable of doing.

A stepparent does not immediately know his step-children's limitations regarding their ability and maturity. He may experience many failures with them, and er-roneously interpret them as an issue of trust. A biological parent, knowing the children's capabilities and limitations, has a greater ability to trust them.

It is important to take the time to identify your step-children's capabilities. You can then show them you trust them in the things you know they can do. If they cannot do something you have asked them to do because it is beyond their ability, it is no longer an issue of trust, but parental misjudgment.

Respect, a vital element of family unity, is an important aspect of acceptance. Some parents make the mistake of trying to force their children to love them, which usually brings disasters.

Respect must be a mutual process. If parents refer to a child by derogatory nicknames, break their promises, show disrespect for his personal possessions and never have time for him, the child will not feel respected and will not offer respect in return. But if parent's sow respect, they will reap respect.

 ## Empathy

Empathy is understanding what someone else is thinking or feeling. It is seeing his world through his eyes.

For a stepparent this means, first of all, having the desire to understand what your stepchild is going through. It means asking Johnny what the tears are all about and listening to what he tells you.

As you listen, hear more than just the words; look at the emotions, the tone of voice and the body language. Is he nervous, depressed, tense, happy? You even have to listen to what is *not* being said. Are there topics he is afraid to discuss—the divorce, your remarriage, sexual issues?

Children's emotions are just as real as those of adults. If Timmy runs into the house bleary-eyed and tells you that his friends won't let him play ball, his problem may seem childish. But the main issue really isn't wanting to play ball, but his sense of rejection, and rejection is a hard feeling to deal with at any age.

As adults it is easy to add our meanings to children's statements and miss the point entirely. An important counseling skill is repeating or summarizing what a client has said. It lets both of us know we are talking about the same thing. This is an important skill you can use with your stepchildren to be sure you understand their perspective.

Genuineness

Children are good at picking out phonies. Suppose Davey asks his stepmother if she is going to his hockey game, and she hates sports. She should be honest (her lack of enthusiasm would soon be evident if she tried to hide her true feelings), but positive. Perhaps she could explain that she has never liked sports because she never understood what was happening. Then she might ask Davey to explain the game to her and let him know she would enjoy sharing his interests. Not only would they be spending valuable time together, but she might even begin to like hockey.

Be real. That doesn't mean you have to "tell all" or express your emotions inappropriately, but you do need to be honest in your relationship.

The skills of acceptance, empathy and genuineness are very important to the bonding process. Without these skills you can participate in numerous activities with your stepchildren, yet bonding may not take place. Bonding occurs in relationship, and relationship occurs between people.

Levels of Accessibility: The Temple

Picture in your mind the floor plans of Solomon's Temple with its outer court, teeming with people and activities; the Holy Place, where only the priests entered; and the Holy of Holies, where only the high priest entered once a year. We can compare accessibility into the different areas of the Temple with entry into a stepchild's life.

The Outer Court: Bonding Through Activities. The outer court of Solomon's Temple was bustling with activity. People were not involved in the spiritual workings of the Temple, but went about daily business. Just as anyone could enter the outer court, so anyone can enter into activities with children. Activities are a "safe" place for stepparent/ stepchild bonding to begin, and a good place for bridge building to intimacy.

Bonding needs to be initiated by the stepparent and should center around the child's interests. The purpose is to put the child into a situation in which he has fun and begins to associate that fun with you. If all the activities you do with your stepchild center around what you want to do, you will be defeating your purpose.

What are your stepchildren involved in that you can go and watch or help them with? Are they playing ball or singing in the choir? What are their interests and what are they doing with those interests? At the same time, what are you doing that they may find interesting? You can plan some activities in advance, like going to the zoo, bowling, visiting a pet shop, seeing a play or getting ice cream together. Attend special events like graduations, recitals or tournaments. These events are important to the stepchildren, which should make them equally important to you.

One of the mistakes parents make when participating in activities with children is thinking the end product of the activity is more important than the time spent together. So what if the kite you built together doesn't stay in the air, or the model airplane isn't perfect? It isn't so much what you do, but what your relationship is like when you do it.

The Holy Place: Bonding Through the Exchange of Ideas. I can visualize an imaginary sign above the doorway of the Temple leading from the outer courts into the Holy Place. It reads: *Priests only. No one else allowed.*

I see basically the same sign posted between a child's activities and his thoughts and feelings: *Friends only. Uncaring people stay out.* A deeper purpose is served by interacting in this realm than in activities, but it is a stepparent's faithfulness in activities that allows him entrance into his stepchild's thoughts.

Once inside, the level of intimacy increases tremendously. The hustle and bustle of activities has given way to a quieter time of two people talking and sharing. If a stepparent is practicing the bonding skills we mentioned earlier, he is in a position to find out what is really going on in his stepchild's mind.

During her junior high years, Nichole went to a school within three blocks of my office. We would meet often for lunch at a restaurant midway between. Nichole told me recently how mature she felt walking into the restaurant, meeting me and eating lunch downtown. While she was impressed with the surroundings, I was impressed with the quality of our conversations. We were sharing honestly and developing a good relationship.

Entrance into Jennifer's thoughts took a different doorway. During our times alone I would sing to her, "Take good care of yourself—you belong to me." Jennifer would reply playfully, "No, you belong to me." I would laugh and say, "No, no. You belong to *me*."

And on we would go. Because Jennifer was so young, we were not at the point of having "intellectually stimulating" conversations. Instead, we bonded by singing songs and spending special times alone together. Now that she is older, we go out for ice cream or plan special times to talk.

Remember, your goal for bonding through the exchange of ideas is not to lecture, but to hear what is going on in your stepchild's life. Your stepchild will pick up on your ideas on his or her own. Just recently, I read an essay Nichole had written and was surprised at how much of me is in my stepdaughter.

The Holy of Holies: Bonding at Its Deepest Level. All the activities in the outer courts and the talks in the Holy Place have been paving the way for the stepparent to enter the heart of the stepchild.

The Old Testament priests entered the Holy of Holies

only once a year for the Day of Atonement. We may have about the same number of appointments to enter the spirit of the child. And even then, they must be given to us. They cannot be planned, pushed or connived. They are special moments when our stepchildren invite us to experience something very meaningful to them—whether joyous or painful.

That afternoon when Nichole unwrapped her cat's Christmas ornament and became upset, I went up to her room to talk with her. After a short time of breaking the ice, I brought Simon into the conversation.

"Your mother told me about Simon's ornament and how much you miss him. You know, Nichole, I'll bet some of those tears were because you miss having your dad living here."

Nichole looked at me, as though wondering whether or not she would be able to talk about it with me.

I continued, "I can understand your feelings. I'd be crying more than you if I were your age and could be with my dad only once a week."

What followed was a conversation from the heart through which we experienced a time of bonding.

Because these opportunities to enter the "Holy of Holies" are infrequent, what you do with them is important. You need to:

> Walk in softly, slowly, and follow your stepchild's leading.
> Be sensitive and realize that the situation and the child's feelings are important.
> Be available. Though it may sound simple, being available is one of the biggest commitments you can make. You can judge your availability by your willingness to put

down the paper, wait to go shopping, or
turn off the football game when your
attention is needed.

Use the bonding skills mentioned earlier.

Be sure your motivation for helping is pure. If
Dennis starts to talk about his mother, don't
use putting her down as an opportunity to
grow closer to Dennis.

Be secure in yourself. Don't feel angry or
threatened when your stepchild talks to
you about your spouse's ex-mate.

How Do You Know When Bonding Has Occurred?

There are several clues that bonding has occurred. These
include: the stepchildren's spontaneous show of affection
and willingness to receive affection; their initiation of conversations and activities; an awareness of your needs; and
asking your opinion.

A spontaneous show of affection may be something that
just happens every now and then. Once in a while you may
get a peck on the cheek, a pat on the back or a heart felt
thank-you.

For some stepchildren (bonded or not) starting a conversation is difficult. It is easier for these children to initiate an
activity, although sometimes in the midst of the activity,
they will loosen up and talk. One stepmother came into my
office thoroughly elated over her stepdaughter's offer to
share an activity with her. "Sharon has asked me to sign up
with her for aerobics at the Y. Isn't that great? I have been
praying for a good relationship with her. Now I'm going to
have to pray for my body!"

A child who is bonding may occasionally show an awareness of his stepparent's physical and emotional needs. He may sense you have had a rough day and ask, "Want to sit down and watch TV with me or something?" Don't expect great displays of self-sacrifice from your stepchildren, but do be aware of their efforts and thoughtfulness.

For me, one sign of my bonding with the girls is when they ask me if I like their hair, or what they are wearing, or if I think some boy is good-looking. By asking my opinion, they are saying that I am a person whose opinion they really want to hear.

When Bonding Does Not Occur

When bonding does not occur, it may be because the people involved do not want it to happen. This unwillingness may be on an unconcious level for some and on a very concious level for others. Anyone may block the bonding process.

Bonding and the Stepparent. There are several reasons why a stepparent may pull away from bonding with his stepchildren.

One is fear of another divorce. This might especially be true if he lost custody of his children through the dissolution of his first marriage. Fear of going through hurt and loss all over again could cause him, even unconsciously, to hold his relationship with his stepchildren at a distance.

Another reason could be guilt over the lost closeness with his own children if they live in another household. He may not feel free to develop close relationships with a new set of children because he cannot spend the time he would like with his own.

A stepparent could also fear his spouse's death and his subsequent separation from the stepchildren. As I began to develop a bonding relationship with Nichole and Jennifer, I became more aware of how my relationship with them would be changed if something were to happen to Adrienne: They would probably go to live with their biological father and I would suffer a triple loss.

Also, a stepparent may not bond if he is jealous of the children's attachment to his spouse. One stepfather had great difficulty bonding. He could not, or would not, let go of his feelings of jealousy about the children's close relationship with their mother. Although it is true his wife was overly attentive to the children, his jealousy only increased the split between the two of them, and drew her and the children even closer together.

One final reason is selfishness. It is difficult for some stepparents to step outside of their own wants, wishes and desires. Due to the self-sacrifice involved, they may never have wanted children. When they married, they considered the children to be solely their mate's responsibility.

What can a stepparent do to stop hindering the bonding process?

First, _realize:_ Love is not limited in quantity. If you give all the love you have today, does that mean you have none left to give tomorrow? If you give all your love to your first child, does that mean there isn't any love left for your second or third child?

Neither is your mate's quantity of love limited. You are both capable of giving yourselves to your children, your stepchildren and to each other. The only limit on love is the limit you set.

Second, _recognize:_ Most things of value come through risk. If you don't risk giving, you'll come up short on receiving. Should you not love your stepchildren today because of something you fear down the road? Absolutely not. If you don't risk loving them today, you have forever lost the joy of the relationship you can have now.

And third, _reciprocate:_ You reap what you sow. This is one principle God has written into the very foundation of the universe. You receive what you give. Even the stepparent who describes his past behavior as selfish and unloving will find his own needs being met in his blended family when he learns to give of himself.

Bonding and the Stepchild. A stepchild may have difficulty bonding because he fears rejection. Children have some of the same fears as adults, but react to them in a childlike fashion. It may be difficult for you to understand why your stepchild would fear your rejection, but he can and often does. Just like you, he doesn't want to go through new hurts.

Your stepchild may also be jealous of your relationship with his biological parent. He could see you as a threat to his relationship with that parent. He may also be jealous of the affection you display toward your biological children and wonder if he will ever receive it.

As a stepchild begins to bond with his stepparent, he may wonder if it is possible to love both his stepparents and biological parents at the same time. In other words, he may feel he is being disloyal to his mother to love his stepmother. In this instance, your stepchild's rejection may have nothing to do with negative aspects of your personality or your ability to fill the parental role. Often the more amiable and understanding the stepparent is, the more intense the loyalty conflict.

One more reason a stepchild may not bond is because of obstinance. He has always had his way and isn't about to give it up. He has learned to manipulate Mom or Dad and the new stepparent poses a real threat to his control in the household. He figures, who wants to bond with the enemy?

How can a stepparent help overcome these obstacles to the bonding process?

First, consistently let your stepchild know you care. Children fear rejection because they have been hurt and are anticipating being hurt again. They need to be reassured over and over again.

Second, don't love your mate and not love his biological children. Again, love is not limited in quantity. Be a family loving one another.

Third, love your stepchildren without competing with the biological parent of the same sex as yourself. I am not the girls' biological father, nor can I replace him. I want Nichole and Jennifer to continue loving their biological father and, because of the freedom they have to love me, he must have communicated the same message.

And last, understand that many times the child we consider to be obstinate is really hurt and discouraged. He has learned to deal with life from a limited perspective, and is afraid to give up the skills he has learned. This child desperately needs someone to believe in him, someone who takes the time to develop a caring relationship.

Bonding and the Biological Parent. A biological parent may block bonding between his mate and his custodial children, first of all, because he fears there might be another divorce and wants to save his children from more emotional trauma.

A second reason is jealousy. He may be jealous of the time his children take his spouse away from him, or he may be jealous of the time his spouse takes his children away from him.

A third reason is the unwillingness of the biological parent to relinquish control and move into co-conducting. In effect the biological parent is saying, "I won't give my spouse any control over my children because she doesn't love them as I do." In order to remain in control, the biological parent must then continue to thwart bonding between the children and their stepparent in order to prove his statement correct.

What can you do as a biological parent if you are a part of your children's difficulty in bonding with their stepparent? There are two important steps.

First, like the stepparent, be aware of your fears and jealousies. Why give up today's joys for the fear of tomorrow's negative possibilities?

Second, remember that if you cling too tightly to your children your mate will not be able to have the influence over them that he needs as co-conductor. Share responsibilities with your mate. It will help you relax about control and let the bonding take place.

Bonding and the Other Household. It is possible for your children's other household to affect bonding in your household. Your spouse's ex-mate may block bonding between you and his biological children because he fears losing his children's affections, especially if he is the non-custodial parent. Or the reason may be hurt and vindictiveness over the divorce.

There is little you can do to change the behavior of the adults in the other household, but you can watch over your own. And you can communicate to the other biological parent that you are not trying to push him out of his children's lives. Children have the capacity to love others for who they are. Bonding with stepparents does not limit their love for their biological parents.

Bonding and the Element of Time

In the movie, *Helen Keller . . . The Miracle Continues,* Helen's suitor asked her, "Do you love me?" Her answer went something like this, "If to love someone means to feel that there are strings attaching your heart to theirs, then I love you."

There will be occasions when you feel you and your stepchild have a connection. Those are the first strands of the bonding process. In time you will weave string upon string and strand upon strand, back and forth between your hearts.

Difficulties arise in blended families when the strings attaching the hearts of the stepparent and stepchild are not very strong before being dealt threatening tugs. An older child, unlike a baby, does not just lie there and soak in the love you offer. He has his own thoughts, past experiences, actions and behavior patterns.

When everything is going smoothly, the stepparent and stepchild feel close. When things are not going well the stepparent and stepchild feel distant. Because only a few strings are attached between them, they have only the current experience to draw them together or push them apart.

Each new caring experience you have attaches another bonding string between your hearts. It takes time to acquire enough strands so that love prevails and circumstances cannot sever the bond.

Patience is one of the virtues stepparents need to practice as they wait for the bonding process to become evident. Earlier, we identified a year-and-a-half to two years as the time necessary for co-conducting to become operational. The time necessary for bonding might be a minimum of a year-and-a-half to two years.

Bonding may become a lengthier process in the case of non-custodial children. Many stepparents have shared with us how difficult it is to bond with stepchildren who come every other weekend, or live out of state and visit once or twice a year. One such stepmother found that by keeping correspondence up with her stepchildren by letters or phone calls, she was able to reestablish closeness with them much quicker when they did come to stay.

Bonding must be intentional. It doesn't just happen. You have to decide you want bonding to occur, then work for it consistently. It means "being there" through activities and emotional crises and realizing that you will probably not receive as much as you give. But be willing to love your stepchildren regardless. The source for that kind of agape love is Jesus. Allow Him to love through you and you will find that agape love supersedes the lack of biological ties.

7

Discipline

"O.K., Frydenger! You're up."

I strolled to home plate, adjusted my cap, raised my bat and took my Babe Ruth stance.

We were down by one run with a man on second. I chomped my bubble gum confidently, and spit.

The outfielders began their chatter, the pitcher stepped up on the mound, paused, and began his windup. The announcer's voice from the loudspeaker hovered over us. "Here's the pitch. It's a strike! Strike one!"

Undaunted I took my stance again in front of home plate.

" . . . And the pitch . . . strike two!"

I was still confident, still chomping my bubble gum and waiting for the perfect pitch. The ball left the pitcher's hand and came racing toward me. A solid crack from my bat indicated a good hit, which the echoing loudspeaker confirmed.

Now came the hard part: getting to first base.

I had a good eye for the ball and could usually put it right where I wanted it, but because of my handicap, running was difficult. I always had a pinch runner, but our Little

League baseball rules required that the batter make it to first base on his own before a pinch runner could take over.

Dropping the bat, I took off for first. However, halfway there my feet became entangled and I tripped and fell flat on my face. I could hear the first base coach shouting toward me, "Come on, Frydenger! Get up! Let's go!" Realizing I could still make it, I struggled to my feet, and stumbled once more. Finally, half-crawling, half-running, with the coach half-crawling, half-running alongside me, I reached first base.

My coach's goal was to get me to first base. When I fell, he didn't run over to punish me for failing, but to encourage me to go on. Parenting should be much the same. Children will take tumbles on their way to mature adulthood. Our job is to encourage them to get up and keep pressing on, not to rush over and scream at them or kick dirt in their faces while they are down. A child has already hurt himself by falling. He doesn't need his parents to inflict additional pain through punishment or verbal abuse.

Parents who view their primary role as one of correcting misbehavior often utilize punishment. Discipline and punishment are not synonymous. When children receive only punishment for falling, they are rarely in a hurry to get back up and try again.

Just like my first base coach, only on a much grander scale, my heavenly Father has a goal for me: to reach Christlike maturity. When I fall, I picture Him watching with loving, rather than judgmental, eyes. When He speaks to me, He says, "Get up, son. Let's go. Don't lie there in the dirt. I love you. Keep moving toward Me." (See Psalm 37:23-24.)

Helping our children grow into mature, responsible Christian adults is our goal as parents. Reaching maturity can be compared to running the bases in a ballgame. The bases might be labeled respect, consequences, self-control and self-imposed accountability.

First Base: Respect for Self and Others

When Nichole and Jennifer feel good about themselves, they understand that my discipline is not a criticism of them as individuals, but a means of changing their behavior. If a child does not feel good about himself, any form of correction becomes a personal threat.

When a child genuinely respects himself, he finds it much easier to respect others. If a child respects himself and not others, he may feel he is better than others, develop a false sense of superiority, and refuse to receive correction from anyone, let alone a stepparent. If, on the other hand, he respects others and not himself, his feelings of unworthiness and his poor self-image will show through in everything he does.

By showing respect to our children and asking for respect in return, we maintain a good atmosphere for healthy growth and fertile ground for effective discipline. Mutual respect is a key ingredient in all learning situations.

Second Base: Consequences

Consequences at home teach children there are consequences for their behavior in life. Some parents, however, either withhold consequences or react disproportionately to the children's behavior. Either one can cause children to develop a false picture of the real world.

Over-protective parents pay for the window Tim broke, blame his teachers for his failing grades, or agree with him about the stupidity of the police officer for giving him a speeding ticket. These parents do Tim a great injustice. He is due for a rude awakening when he is no longer under their protective care.

Punitive parents are on the other end of the continuum. They give their children consequences that are too severe in relation to the misconduct. If Missy is ten minutes late getting back from a date, Missy can't date for three months.

Inconsistent parents switch from no consequences to severe consequences that are unrelated to the child's misbehavior, leaving the child confused.

Ideally, the consequences a child experiences in his home reflect the natural, environmental and social order in which we live, and are directly related to his behavior.

Third Base: Self-Control

Children who have never faced consistent consequences for misbehavior in their family structures may display little or no self-control. These children are not concerned about punishment and could care less about appropriate or inappropriate behavior. Too often I have seen children who are "perfect little darlings" in the controlling presence of their parents explode into gross misbehavior in their parents' absence.

We cannot externally control our children until they are eighteen and then expect them to turn on some internal switch of self-control. Nor can we expect a child who has grown up without restraints and always done as he pleases to make wise choices in adulthood.

Children gain self-control when they are given the freedom to make choices and face the consequences for those choices. Self-control is learned. Just like playing the piano or shooting baskets, it takes practice.

Home Plate: Willingness to be Accountable for Your Actions

It is impossible to score at home plate without first touching the other three bases. It is equally impossible to reach self-imposed accountability without respect, an understanding of consequences and self-control.

If you ask a child to be accountable for himself before he touches all the bases he might well answer:

First base
without respect for himself: "I'm afraid to."
without respect for others: "Why should I have to?"

Second base
without an understanding of consequences: "How can I be held accountable when the whole world is against me? I'm just unlucky. . . ."

Third base
without self-control: "Why should I be held accountable for what I did? Someone else made me do it."

We eventually want our children to be able to say, "I am responsible for my actions, my emotions, my relationships and my life." A young person reaching true maturity not only submits himself to society-imposed regulations, but also imposes discipline upon himself. Such discipline may include things like daily Bible reading, academic study, exercise or characteristics like honesty and integrity.

If my first base coach had been like an over-protective parent, he would have hovered over me when I went to bat, followed my every move as I ran and rushed to pick me up and carry me to first base when I fell. By doing everything for our children, we rob them of experiences that will help them grow and develop.

If he had been like an authoritarian or judgmental parent, he would have expelled me when I failed and banned me from playing in any more games. A parent's job is to coach and encourage his children to try again.

If he had been like a permissive parent, he would have run onto the field, tackled the player who caught my hit and held him down until I made it to first base. The parent who will not establish logical consequences and who blocks natural consequences is much like a coach who interferes with a play on the field.

Chances are that one mate will be permissive (usually the biological mother) and the other mate will be authoritarian (usually the stepfather). In order for the children in a blended family to make it around the bases to home plate, both parents must be co-conductors—parent and step-parent working together toward the same goal in their children's lives.

Communication with Your Mate

Often couples who have expressed their opinions to one another think they have communicated. That is not necessarily so. Teresa and Frank, for instance, each expressed their concern for her son, Jason, about bike riding in the street. Teresa wanted Jason to stay on the sidewalk and Frank felt he was old enough to start learning to watch out for himself.

When Teresa returned home one day to find Jason riding his bike in the street she stormed into the house, furious with Jason's stepfather.

"Frank," she charged, "I thought we talked about Jason riding his bike in the street!"

"That's right," replied Frank. "We did. You told me you didn't want Jason riding his bike in the street and I told you I thought he was old enough."

Obviously Teresa and Frank had not really communicated. You need to talk *and* listen to each other—particularly about discipline. Remember that there are differences between mates in personality, male/female differences in child-rearing, and a difference in the kind of discipline each one experienced as a child. Then, add to these differences the years that one or both parents spent making all the decisions in a single-parent household and the need to decide "right now" what is acceptable behavior. The problems are compounded when the children decide to pick up on parental discrepancies and use them to pit parents and stepparents against each other.

Often, parents can become so involved in arguing about their differences, they forget the issue of their debate—the children's behavior. When they can come to an agreement through open communication, they can bring the children's "divide and conquer" tactics to a halt. Unity between mates allows them to send out clear messages to the children.

The Bible very clearly states that a house divided against itself will fall (Mark 3:25). If parent and stepparent can't agree on how to raise Tony and Melissa they will be engaged in an unending tug of war over discipline. If they agree on one direction and pull together, however, they will not only develop a creative, positive atmosphere, but they will begin praying in agreement.

Jesus made a powerful statement about being in agreement: "Again, I tell you that if two of you on earth agree about anything you ask for, it will be done for you by my Father in heaven" (Matthew 18:19). To think we can unleash the power of God into the lives of our children simply by being in unity with one another is mind-boggling.

Agreement on Expectations

If parents are locked in disagreement over children, they may appear to be fighting for different goals.

One assignment I often give to parents in blended families, with surprising results, is the Expectation List. I ask both parents to list the expectations they have for each child, including grades and study habits, personal hygiene, household responsibilities, manners, dress, social skills, spiritual life, music, TV-viewing, friends and sleeping habits.

Shared expectations are important. They give the parent and stepparent a unity of purpose as they relate to their children. You and your mate will want to sit down and list the expectations for each child in your blended family, compare your lists and find where your expectations are shared.

Invariably parents are surprised at the similarities. Typically, one says, "I can't believe this. She wants the same things for the children as I do. All this time I thought we were arguing because she thought I expected too much, and I thought she expected too little."

For the first year of blended family life, major differences in expectations should be deferred to the biological parent's wishes. Later on, a blending of both the parent's and stepparent's expectations needs to take place.

Agreement on Means

Even though "easing in the co-conductor" may be in operation from day one of your remarriage, there are always immediate child-rearing decisions that have to be made. And at the time of the wedding, the children have had a lot more experience at manipulating parents than you and your spouse have had at parenting together. After determining expectations, you have to determine the means. This may take some negotiating since both parents may have different ideas about implementing discipline.

If Adrienne and I both agree we don't want our children to burp at the dinner table, our next step is to decide how to correct that behavior. When our children burp at the table, are we going to:

> Scream at them?
> Thump them on the head?
> Embarrass them in front of others at the table?
> Have them sit in the corner and eat alone?
> Remove their food?
> Tell them they may eat with the family when they
>   decide not to burp at the dinner table, and
>   until then they are excused from the room?

As a stepparent I need to know which of these means is acceptable to Adrienne, which ones she has tried, and which one gave her the most success. If up to this point, none of them has been successful, which one is she willing to try again?

Mates in a remarriage may have difficulty negotiating their means of discipline for fear of entering into open combat in that marriage as they did in the last one. But even if they remain silent, their thoughts and actions may speak louder than any battle cry:

If she's not going to make these kids mind, I will.
Boy, is he being tough on the kids. I'd better ease up a little.
They get away with murder around her. They're not going to get away with anything around me!

When mates do not discuss their differences openly in discipline, they begin to move in opposite directions in their means. Picture a man and a woman in a tug of war. Between them is a marker denoting middle ground. As each tries to pull the other to the middle ground, they are actually straining toward opposite ends, moving farther away from their mutual goals. Neither one moves any closer to the middle. They just keep stretching the rope, pulling it tighter, putting a strain on their relationship.

This movement to opposite ends of the continuum is a typical pattern when there is a lack of communication between mates. What may have started out as a small difference of opinion becomes full-blown opposition.

The ability to make discipline decisions right away is especially critical when two sets of children live in the same household and when both mates have developed their own means of discipline from heading single-parent households. Changes in both the expectations for the children and the means of discipline will have to be made right away in order to establish unity and fairness and to guard against feelings of animosity. Usually it is the single mother who tends to put discipline on the back burner and becomes increasingly permissive. When Stepdad joins the family, he can see the lack of discipline and is all too ready to put discipline on the front burner and apply heat.

It is important to be specific when communicating and

negotiating about discipline. Generalized statements like "Sammy has been a real brat today" are too broad to negotiate. What were the specific behaviors which led to that statement? Did Sammy talk back, stomp out of the room, slam the door, ignore you? What specifically did Sammy do?

As you talk with your mate about Sammy's behavior, make sure Sammy is not present. Children need not hear the negotiation, only the conclusion. Discuss one behavior at a time (e.g., talking back) and jointly determine how you are going to respond to that specific behavior. Attacking all of Sammy's misbehaviors at once is not only unproductive, but leads to anger and defensiveness on the part of the biological parent.

Negotiating to agreement is vitally important for the discipline of the children in your blended family. In order to make the high level of commitment necessary for discipline to be effective you both need to feel you had a part in establishing the means. Remember a basic point: If you don't like the program, you won't follow it.

Communicate with Your Children. As a child, I promised myself I would never tell *my* children, "Do it because I said so." It has slipped out of my mouth on one or two occasions and, believe me, it is not a productive phrase for discipline. Children should know the rules, consequences and rationale of your discipline.

There are few things more defeating than playing a game when you don't know the rules. When I was in the sixth grade, I lost my entire life's savings to some older, more worldly boys in our neighborhood. They talked me into playing poker, taught me how to play, and walked off with my three dollars. To this day, I am convinced they kept changing the rules.

Children have described this feeling to me in regard to

discipline and new rules that landed them in household solitary confinement for actions they didn't know were criminal. Children need to have the program laid out in front of them well in advance of their misbehavior.

Just as you need to talk in specific terms with your mate, so you need to talk in specific terms with the children in your blended family. When you tell your child to "straighten up," you and he may have different opinions of what straightening up means.

He may not understand what terms like *obnoxious* or *disrespectful* imply. But he does understand statements like, "You are not to slam the receiver when I ask you to get off the phone." In being concrete, you state your expectations and consequences in equally clear, identifiable terms.

Discipline Through Consequences

The happy medium between discipline that is merely punishment and discipline that is too lenient is teaching your child about consquences.

Natural consequences are the result of action or behavior when nature is allowed to run its course. Children sometimes don't take the course of nature into consideration. For instance, how many times have you argued with one of your children over wearing a jacket and had it go something like this:

"Boris, you are going to wear this jacket."

"I am not. I'll get too hot."

"It isn't that warm outside."

"Yes, it is."

"No, it isn't! I am your mother and you are going to wear this jacket."

A few minutes later Boris walks out the door wearing his jacket.

To use natural consequences in this situation, his mother would have allowed him to make a choice following the suggestion that he wear a jacket because it was cold outside. If he refused to wear it, his mother wouldn't harangue him by telling him what a bad choice he made. She would simply say, "O.K.," and let him go outside and face the natural consequence of his behavior—getting cold.

Once outside, one of his friends might ask him, "Hey, where's your jacket? You look like you're freezing!" At that point, Boris would know he was the one responsible for not wearing a jacket, not his mother. The use of consequences moves the responsibility of the child's behavior from the parent to the child.

When using natural consequences, your responsibility is to offer your child an appropriate choice. Then stand back and let the consequences happen. If Boris refuses to wear a coat, he will get cold.

This doesn't mean you are not considerate of your children. It doesn't mean you don't care that Boris is cold. It does mean that you are interested in teaching him that there are realities in life and that you want him to grow into a mature and responsible adult.

Logical consequences are different from natural consequences in that they must be designed and imposed by parental authority. They are called logical because they are logically related to the misbehavior. If Freddy loses your hammer, don't ground him for a month. Have him buy a new hammer out of his allowance.

Or if the weather really is cold enough for Boris to catch pneumonia, the natural consequence would be too severe. In that case, it is up to Mom or Dad to impose a logical consequence: "Boris, you can either wear your jacket and play outside or stay in the house where it is warm."

The way the logical consequences are imposed makes a

difference in their effectiveness. Don Dinkmeyer and Gary D. McKay have a program written for parents entitled *Systematic Training for Effective Parenting* (STEP). The three steps they suggest in applying consequences are as follows:

Step One: "Provide choices. Choice is essential in the use of logical consequences. Alternatives are proposed by the parent and the parent accepts the child's decision. Then the child makes a choice without external pressure. The parent's tone of voice is crucial. It must reflect an attitude of respect, acceptance and good will. The choice of words is also important."[1] For example: "Jennifer, you must remember to put your new bicycle in the garage at night or you will lose the privilege of riding it the next day."

Step Two: "As you follow through with a consequence, give assurance that there will be an opportunity to change the decision later. After you give children a choice, they often decide to test the limits. When this happens, tell them that the decision stands, but they may try again later."[2] For example: "I see you did not put your bicycle away last night, Jennifer. You may not ride it today, but you may ride it again tomorrow."

Step Three: "If the misbehavior is repeated, extend the time that must elapse before the child may try again. If children continue to misbehave, they are saying they aren't ready to be responsible."[3] For example: "I see you decided not to put your bicycle away again last night, Jennifer. You may not ride it for two days."

Each time the same misbehavior occurs, extend the time.

[1] Don Dinkmeyer and Gary D. McKay, *Systematic Training for Effective Parenting (STEP)*, Parents Handbook, American Guidance Service, Inc., Circle Pines, Minn., 1976., p. 77.

[2] Ibid.

[3] Ibid.

The next time Jennifer leaves her bicycle out, she will not be able to ride it for three days, then four days, then five days. Increase by single increments, not double or triple.

It is important to separate the act from the person. If a child spills his milk, that doesn't make him a "bad boy." Your statements should be limited to the act or the behavior. Remember to see each child in your blended family as an individual. Consequences should not only be logically related, but take into account the personality of the child.

If both the biological parent and stepparent use natural and logical consequences, positive things can happen.

When natural consequences are used, there is an automatic fairness in the way the parent and stepparent treat all the children. By allowing the children to face natural consequences, the parent and stepparent are not imposing anything; nature is.

Because the husband and wife have discussed and come to an agreement on what consequences are logical for specific behaviors, a relationship of fairness between them can develop.

The children will complain less about unfairness.

Due to agreement between parent and stepparent, children cannot utilize the "divide and conquer" technique.

Swift, direct action can be used in misbehavior situations. There is no need to wait for the biological parent to get home if both parents use natural and agreed upon logical consequences.

As time goes on, the children will begin to see the

rules as family rules rather than stepparent versus biological parent rules.

A genuine display of respect between parent, stepparent and child can develop. The parent and stepparent show respect for the children by offering choices and accepting their decisions. The parents earn the children's respect by not responding with anger, by being consistent in discipline and by refusing to argue.

Giving children choices with follow-up consequences encourages independence by allowing them to practice the decision-making process.

When children are not bribed to be good or act good, they can appreciate the feeling of responsibility as its own reward.

Consistency

Being consistent with your children is important to every relationship in your blended family. Imagine the following situation.

On Monday, Evelyn prepared beef stroganoff for the evening meal. As the family sat down to eat, her son Kevin walked up to the table, spied the stroganoff and remarked, "Not that stuff again! I don't like it."

With her husband's backing, Evelyn replied, "Kevin, if you don't want to eat what I have prepared for supper, you don't have to. But there will be no eating until breakfast."

"O.K., I won't eat." Kevin left the dining room and went out to play.

Later, despite his whining, moaning and groaning about imminent death if he didn't have at least a couple cookies, Eveyln allowed Kevin to face the natural consequence of not eating dinner—hunger. He ate a good breakfast the next morning.

On Tuesday, Evelyn made chicken cacciatore for supper. This time Kevin was happy, but his stepbrother, Philip, was not. "What is this? I don't want to eat this stuff."

Evelyn calmly reminded her stepson that refusing to eat was his choice—"but you will not eat again until breakfast." As Philip left the dinner table, Philip's father seemed to be in complete agreement with her.

Later in the evening Philip began moaning that he was starving, only to find Evelyn sticking to her word. At 8:00, however, Evelyn walked into the kitchen and found Philip's father fixing dinner for him.

"The boy's really hungry, Evelyn," he said. "He has to keep his strength up for track, you know."

How do you suppose Evelyn felt? How would you feel? And how would Kevin have felt, after suffering through hunger pangs the night before, if he had walked in on stepdad cooking his stepbrother a big, juicy burger?

Consistency is a must in your couple relationship. There are always exceptions to the rule if you look for them; don't look for them. Follow the rules you and your mate agreed upon.

Inconsistency can be confusing for children. Granted, no one is completely consistent. If you and your mate have agreed on a program of natural and logical consequences, however, and work on sticking with it, there will be less chance that either of you will just react to misbehavior and a greater chance for consistent discipline.

Control

When you begin using natural and logical consequences, you are still in control. Your children make choices from the ones you offer them. A ten-year-old does not have the choice of whether or not to drive the car because you don't offer him that choice. It is our job as parents and stepparents to set up the boundaries our children are to live within.

The goal of discipline is to pass control from the parent to the child in the appropriate amount at the appropriate age. Some parents and stepparents panic when I tell them they need to allow their children to have more control over their own lives. I sometimes panic myself, but because I want my children to be able to control themselves whether Adrienne and I are present or not, I have to let loose of my children and my panic.

Sailing the Seven "C's"

In summary, we would like you to think of this chapter in terms of "Sailing the seven 'C's' of discipline." To help you remember the basics, remember the following seven words.

Communication. One of the marriage-saving ingredients in blended families is agreement through communication. Always talk things over.

Concreteness. State all communication in specific terms, whether it involves expectations, consequences or standards. With clear, concrete communication, there is little room for misunderstanding.

Commitment. A good discipline program requires commitment. A higher level of commitment is assured when everyone involved clearly understands the program.

Choice. Enable the children in your blended family to practice the decision-making process by allowing them to choose from the options you provide.

Consequences. Choices result in consequences. Allow the children to face natural and logical consequences which are directly related to their behavior.

Consistency. Consistent parenting lets your children know what to expect. When they know what to expect, they can make more responsible decisions. Consistency in dealing with the children also improves the husband and wife relationship.

Control. Parents need to be in control, but must allow their children to grow in their ability to control themselves. Your goal as a parent is to give control to them at appropriate age levels, and eventually to relinquish control completely.

8

Working With the Other Household

As I work with blended families I am repeatedly amazed at the number of problems they have with their other households. The biological parents continue to fight as much after their divorce as they did when they were married. There is often an ongoing attempt at manipulation; the children are used as bullets in the war games; and revenge takes higher precedence than the children's welfare.

It is much easier for a couple without children to make a complete break following a divorce than it is for a couple with children. Children born in a first marriage always tie the divorcing parents together. That relationship can be disastrous for both households when the biological parents see each other as ex-mates, instead of their children's other parent.

Jerry and Bonnie came to talk with me for just such relationships with their other households. As they explained it, Jerry was frustrated at his ex-wife's attempts to turn their three sons against him.

"Stella is bitter," he explained, "and she never says *anything* positive to the boys about me. She tries to cut their visitation time short or makes excuses why they can't come at all.

"And the way Stella is raising the boys!" he said, leaning forward in his seat. "They're allowed to run all over town on their bikes. Then she leaves Danny, who is only eleven, home to babysit for the other two while she goes out shopping.

"I never know what my children are doing from one day to the next and that bothers me all the time. I have no control over what is happening in their lives. I'm not raising my children. I feel I have very little input in their value systems."

People like Jerry want to get over the hurts and get on with life, providing a healthy atmosphere for all the children to grow up in. The difficulties Jerry describes come from a common problem: Stella still sees Jerry as her ex-mate, not as the boys' father. Instead of working to separate her children from Jerry's household, Stella should have been working on separating herself from Jerry.

A psychological and emotional divorce must accompany the legal divorce. If it does not occur, as in Stella's case, anger and bitterness between the biological parents will spill over into both households and make everybody's lives miserable. A distinct boundary has to be drawn between the adults in both households, but not between the children and the adults. Stella must recognize that her children are very much a part of the other household, though she is not.

Conflicts Between Households

Any number of conflicts can develop between households. As varied as these difficulties may be, they can usually be traced to two basic root causes.

The first is unresolved feelings from the previous marriage. These feelings may include anger, unforgiveness or still feeling in love with the ex-mate.

The second is personality traits. Although the marriage ended, the ex's behavior has not. He may still be a procrastinator or a workaholic. She may still be insecure or a hypochondriac.

Some of the conflicts arising between households may come from a combination of the two. Some of the more specific problems are as follows:

Negative comments the other biological parent makes about you or your mate in front of the children. Comments that start in the other household and filter down to you may go something like this.

"Mom said you ran out on us because you don't love me."

"Dad said we couldn't do anything last weekend because he spends all of his money paying for everything over here."

(Addressed to stepdad) "Do you know how to play football? My dad said you probably don't even know what a football is."

One father related to us how it felt to hear his children ask him about the "sordid details" of relationships he never had. He said that even though his first reaction was to get even and "tell what really happened" he was able to respond calmly. "Somehow or other," he said, "I managed to straighten the story out without calling their mother a liar or telling them the things she did. That had to be the grace of God!"

Another stepfather told us how his four-year-old stepson relayed a message from his biological father. "My dad said you can't spank me. If you do, I'm supposed to tell him, and he'll beat you up. What are you going to do?"

The stepfather chose not to address the challenge made

by the biological father. Instead, he just answered the boy's question. "Well, if you need to be spanked, I'll spank you." To which his stepson replied, "Oh, O.K."

The first temptation when you hear negative comments being directed toward your household is to strike back with a bigger, better blow. Don't give in to that temptation. If the children are being led to believe a falsehood, correct it by telling the truth without attacking the other parent or making retaliatory remarks.

Biological parents blaming each other for problems the children have. Biological parents may continue to attack each other by making comments about the children to the children.

"I'll tell you why you're getting such lousy grades. It's because your mother is too self-centered to sit down with you and help you with your homework."

"You wouldn't be so fat if your mother fed you right."

"You wouldn't be afraid of men if your father had stayed around and taught you how to get along with them."

Such comments are doing just as much damage to the child as the real or imagined faults of the other parent. This kind of parental warfare only teaches the child not to accept responsibility for his own actions by placing the blame on someone else.

Even if the children are not present, parents aren't helping anything by blaming each other for their children's problems. Concentrate your energies on what you can do to help your child, not on who you can blame.

Visitation Conflicts. Visitation is an important issue for the children. Their needs should be the primary determinate in resolving visitation conflicts.

Very young children should not be required to leave their custodial home for an extended period of time. Children up to age four should not be expected to spend the night away from their custodial households. The amount of time spent in the non-custodial household after the age of six really depends on the quality of the ongoing relationship between the non-custodial parent and the child. The stability of the non-custodial parent and his or her parenting skills should all be taken into consideration when working out visitation schedules.

Visitation should not be so frequent that it disrupts the establishment of a routine in the custodial household. Visitation itself should be established as a routine. It should be something the children can look forward to and plan on. As the children grow older, an already established routine can be helpful when they begin planning their own outside activities.

The responsibility for visitation should not be left up to small children by either the custodial or non-custodial parent. It is unfair to expect eight-year-old Brian to call you when he wants to see you. That would require too much responsibility. Besides, Bryan might begin questioning your love for him. "Doesn't Dad [or Mom] ever want to see me?"

One father who decided to try this kind of visitation arrangement soon went back to initiating visitation. "I became tired of Jeremy turning me down when I would call and ask if we could get together. When we reversed the procedure, I found myself saying no to Jeremy on several occasions. Now we're back to my calling him. I have the bigger shoulders to handle disappointment."

Some offices have a standing policy for no-show appointments. If a client misses his appointment without giving a twenty-four hour cancellation notice, a charge is added to his bill. If some children were to adopt the same policy with their non-custodial parent, they would collect almost enough to pay for their first year of college.

Shane's father was a no-show parent. Early in the week

he told Shane, "I'll pick you up this Saturday around noon and we'll do a little fishing, just you and me. We may even fry them up that night for supper."

When Saturday came, Shane was ready with his tackle box and fishing pole by ten o'clock. Every time the phone rang or a car would go by Shane would yell, "That's Dad!" It wasn't until five o'clock that Shane finally gave up and put his fishing gear away. That happened three weekends in a row, until finally Shane lost hope that his father would ever follow through.

No-show parents are not always non-custodial parents. There are custodial parents who arrange to have the children's other parent pick them up for the day, and then disappear for the weekend.

What is the other parent's responsibility for these no-show moms and dads? Parents often ask me whether they should lie or make excuses or let the kids know how irresponsible their other parent really is.

Actually, neither. Be honest, but don't be cruel. In Shane's case, "Dad apparently forgot; we'll get a hold of him later" is sufficient. Don't say, "Your dad's probably out drinking," or, "He's probably having so much fun he forgot to pick you up." A child will eventually form his own ideas about an irresponsible parent. He doesn't need your assistance.

There are situations in which you can prepare for possible failure on the part of your child's other parent. If the parent is usually a no-show, for example, be ready for him in the event he *does* show up, but don't tell the children he's coming until he pulls in the driveway. On the other hand, don't take responsibility for that parent by constantly calling him and reminding him what day he is to visit.

Another question parents ask is, "What do I do when I hear or see my child being manipulated by his other parent about visitation?" One mother with two girls in their teens told us how their father responded to a planned visit in his home.

The girls telephoned their father to let him know they planned to spend one day of the upcoming holiday with their grandmother, then three days with him, and back home in time for an activity with their church youth fellowship. But when their dad heard how long they were planning on staying, he replied angrily, "If you can't stay longer than three days, don't bother to come at all!" and hung up.

When you hear your children being manipulated, help them to recognize it as manipulation. Again, this does not require negative comments about their other parent, just about the manipulation. The mother of the two girls didn't tell them how rotten their father was. Instead she identified the process. The girls were then able to see how their dad's comment was meant to make them feel guilty in order to force them to spend more time with him.

In some blended families, visitation has been clearly defined by the courts, including the exact times the children are to be picked up and brought home. Holidays and summer vacations are locked in.

Other households have what is termed "reasonable visitation," which means the schedules are flexible. Teenagers in these households should always be consulted about visitation plans. They have activities outside of both households that need to be taken into consideration. Although younger children do not need to be consulted, they do need to be aware of the plans. Jennifer, who is ten, likes to know which day of the weekend she is going to visit her other household so she can make plans to do things with her friends in the neighborhood on the other day.

Our household follows reasonable visitation scheduling. In order to make that work well, it is very important to communicate with the other household when making plans concerning weekends, visiting the extended family in the other household, holidays and vacations.

One of our goals in utilizing a flexible schedule is to maximize the time the girls spend with their biological father. If Jennifer or Nichole has an activity on the day they are to visit their other household, we offer to change days. For example, we may ask, "Do you want the girls to come Saturday and take Jennifer to her Brownie meeting, or do you want them to come Sunday?"

Children's activities can cause problems between households. In Jerry's case, Stella was adamant he take the boys to every activity she planned for them. Jerry felt Stella was using the activities to diminish his time with his sons and balked at the idea, until he found a solution that seemed to settle it with Stella.

One evening Jerry and his new wife went to pick the boys up for a two-week vacation. When they arrived, Stella handed him a long list of activities for the boys, including a four-day tournament. Stella was clearly showing that she did not want the boys to relax and enjoy their time in the other household, and that she did not want Jerry and Bonnie to be able to enjoy having them.

Jerry looked at the list, folded it up, put it in his pocket and stood up to leave. "All right," he said. "We don't want to interfere with your plans for the boys. We'll take them for three days, bring them back here for the four-day tournament, and pick them up after the tournament is over to finish out our vacation."

Stella, who had plans of her own for the next two weeks, was stunned. "You can't do that. You have to take them for the whole two weeks."

When Jerry held his ground, she understood that she

could no longer try and manipulate the other household with the children's activities.

Using the Children as Bullets; or, Ready, Aim, Fire! Children are sometimes used as ammunition to take pot shots at the other household. You need to realize, however, that your children are not strong enough for that; they will be damaged upon impact.

Some parents attacks are so obvious that even the children can see them coming. One example, as incredible as it seems, is the father who tape-recorded his seedy interpretation of what went on between the children's mother and stepfather before they were married, and then played it for his children.

Most attacks are not as obvious. You have no idea you are in danger until you feel the pain. These techniques include disciplining in a way that affects the other household, pumping the kids for information, and undermining authority in the other household.

Don't discipline your children in a way that affects the other household. If your children misbehave, don't send them to their rooms just when the non-custodial parent is due to arrive. If Michelle acts up one minute before dad comes, let her know she will experience the consequence for her behavior when she returns. Enforce that consequence when Michelle comes home, even if you have to write it down to remember it.

If a child is grounded, you cannot ground him from visiting his other household, nor can you enforce that grounding while he is there. You can inform the other household that your child is grounded and why, but it is up to them to determine how they are going to respond.

Anyone trying to keep children as far away as possible from their other household can rationalize any behavior.

For example, you may threaten: "If you keep this up, young man, you won't be going over to your dad's this weekend." Now you have stated a consequence. You may rationalize, "To be a good parent I have to follow through. Right?" Not right. The fact is, you should never have made the threat in the first place.

Some parents pump their children for news about the other household. They try to get information by "priming the pump" with questions like: "Did Mommy get a job yet?" (which really means, "Is she working so I can reduce my support payment?"); "Does Daddy have anything new at the house?" (which really means, "The tightwad didn't buy me anything when we were married. I'll bet he's blowing all his money now"); "Was anybody else there when you visited Daddy?" (which really means, "Is he dating anybody yet? What does she look like? Were they acting romantic?").

If you want to know what is happening in the other household, ask the other household, not your children. Pumping your children for information indicates there has not been an emotional or psychological separation between households.

Another way of attacking the other household is by undermining its authority. It is one thing to be protective of your children and not want them to be severely punished. It is another thing entirely to encourage your children to act any way they want in their other household because you will block the consequences.

Different Values and Standards

Every home has its own set of values. Even in households with the same moral philosophy, peripheral issues may differ. One household may value athletic competition while another disdains it. The work ethic may be high priority in one home while cleanliness has high priority in another. Many other values—academic excellence, diet, personal hygiene or discipline—may become issues that cause concern between households.

Perhaps you are thinking: "Those differences I can handle. But what about moral issues?" One father said neighbors were constantly impressed with the way his children helped their custodial mother around the house. While he was pleased with his children's work, he said he was more concerned about their learning to tell the truth and having good values than cutting the grass and carrying in groceries.

Here are some of the moral issues parents and stepparents have expressed concern about:

Cheating, lying and stealing. Because each of these behaviors is rewarding in itself, children need parental authority to provide consequences for these behaviors.

Television viewing. Even prime-time television has its share of profanity, sex and violence. Pay cable television offers programs that should not be viewed by adults, let alone children.

Availability of pornographic literature and videos. The question parents ask is, "What is going into my child's mind, and what kind of sexual/moral standard is he developing in his other household?"

Use of alcohol and drugs. Even if the other household does not permit the children to use them, they may see role models there who may use or abuse alcohol or drugs.

Sexual activity outside of marriage. Dad or Mom having a friend over to spend the night is of great concern to many parents who are trying to teach their children a biblical perspective on sex and marriage.

Abortion. Abortion is one of the key moral issues of this age. Many parents do not want their children exposed to a role model who supports the killing of unborn babies.

Homosexuality. Because sexual orientation is a choice, many parents do not want their children exposed to this "alternate lifestyle" that is described biblically as sin.

Use of profanity. The use of profanity has invaded every social class and every media. Again, parents are concerned about having their children around a role model who makes use of profanity in even casual conversation.

The occult. The ouija board, seances, horoscopes, palm reading, while seen by some as playful entertainment, are recognized by others as demonic tools in opposition to Christianity.

Parents with high moral standards ask what they can do about sending their children into what they feel is an immoral atmosphere. Legally, they cannot keep their children home or terminate visitation unless they can prove abuse, neglect or long-term psychological damage to the children. In other words, unless the activities are illegal, parents cannot regulate what is taking place in their children's other household.

This is where parents' use of logical and natural consequences is most helpful. Even though these parents cannot control the other household, or their children while they are in the other household, they can help their children learn to make decisions. Remind your children of the things you don't approve of in your household, and that you don't approve of them in the other household, either, and add,"Remember, you are responsible for your own actions."

Even though you have no control over the other household, you can let the adults know what your standards are, if you communicate them in a positive way. For example, if Sally has nightmares after watching a horror movie at her other household, don't call and berate the other parents for being insensitive to Sally. Instead, you could call and say, "Sally has been having terrible nightmares and I think it is because of the horror movies she's been watching. I was wondering if you would monitor the programs she watches on television while she's there, and I'll do the same here."

If you are facing different standards and values (or even if you aren't), try following these ideas:

Set a good example by living a Christian life in front of your children.

Teach your children to be responsible for their own actions by using natural and logical consequences.

Pray for your children and for the other household. We know of many cases where prayer has changed situations and relationships. Trust God to perform His work in your children's lives. Don't underestimate His power.

Legal Issues

We are often asked questions that are more legal than psychological. An Illinois attorney and I discussed the following questions to offer a legal perspective. (Several answers refer to Illinois state law, and you will need to check the laws of your state for specifics.)

"My ex hasn't been paying child support. Can I keep him from seeing the children?" or *"My wife is not following the visitation agreement. Can I stop paying child support?"*
No to both questions. Child support and visitation are absolutely independent of each other. One is not granted or denied, paid or not paid, because of what the other parent does or does not do. If one does not pay support as ordered, one can go to jail for up to six months, even if visitation has been consistently denied. One can also go to jail for denying visitation, even if child support has not been paid. Jail is the ultimate penalty for failure to follow court orders.

"Should I as a custodial parent go after overdue child-support payments?"
Certainly. Several mechanisms exist for collection of support. The non-payer can be reached out of state as well as within. Some support collection services are free.

"Who pays those court and attorney fees?"
In Illinois and other states, courts are required by law to award attorney's fees to the person who has to sue to collect back support. If the person being sued is already in contempt of court (i.e., withholding visitation or child support), he is responsible for all court and attorney fees. A finding of contempt is made when it is shown to the court's

satisfaction that the non-payer deliberately violated the court's order to pay support.

"My ex-husband was angry over the amount he was ordered by the court to pay for child support and quit his job. Now what do I do?"

If one voluntaily reduces one's income, the courts will not grant relief from support obligations. If one suffers an involuntary reduction in income, courts will ordinarily offer some relief from support. For example:

"I quit my job." No reduction. Support accumulates at court-ordered rate.

"I was fired through no fault of my own." Support will most likely be reduced to an amount commensurate with present income.

"I was laid off." Support will often equal the allotment paid by unemployment compensation for the support of dependents.

"I'm on strike." This is voluntary. Two approaches can be taken. Either support is abated during the strike or support is suspended, meaning it accumulates at a regular rate but is not payable until after the return to work.

It would be highly unusual to have the support obligation lifted. If the non-custodial parent has *any* income, some percentage must be paid for support.

"As a non-custodial parent, what do I do if my children are ill and their custodial parent does not take them to a doctor? Do I have the right to take them? What about psychological testing?"

If a child is seriously ill, the non-custodial parent should take the child for care without thought for "rights" to do so. Any custodial parent would be laughed out of court if he or she tried to show that the care should not have been obtained.

It is the custodial parent's right and responsibility to
obtain general or routine physical or psychological care. If
the non-custodial parent perceives a need for some care
that is not being received, he or she may petition the court
for an order directing that physical or psychological care be
given.

If it appears that care is being denied, the non-custodial
parent should keep a notebook recording date, time, place
and nature of each occurrence. If the custodial parent cannot be persuaded when confronted with the facts, then the
notebook will be invaluable in preparing evidence for court.

*"If the non-custodial parent's visits are irregular or inconsis-
tent, can visitation be terminated?"*
No. The courts consistently take the position that visitation is an absolute right. Denial of visitation by a parent
amounts to a punishable contempt of court. There are
certain circumstances in which courts will restrict or deny
visitation, but usually only in cases of possible harm or
danger to the children.

Parenthetically, I have observed that when visitation is
irregular or inconsistent it is because the custodial parent
makes it so difficult and unpleasant.

*"If the non-custodial parent refuses to take one of the children on
visitations, can the other children be withheld?"*
This question is more philosophical than legal. Why
would visitation be denied? Would that be good for the
child? Are there reasons that the non-custodial parent visits
only with certain children? Is it better for the children to
have serial rather than group visitation? Are children the
property of the custodial parent to be withheld at whim?
What is the goal here?

So often visitation problems are a direct result of the

relationship of the ex-mates—probably 99.9 percent of the time. The child who is not visited is often the closest to the custodial parent and may be extremely hostile to the non-custodial parent. Family therapy is a better alternative than court action.

"If you have been afraid the non-custodial parent might skip town with the children, and then they are late getting home one evening, what do you do? How long do you wait to report it? Who do you report it to?"

First, go to the non-custodial parent's house and see if the children are there. Also check with his or her relatives and close friends. When you are as certain as you can reasonably be that they are not in town, call the police.

Removing children from the custodial parent without permission of the parent or the court constitutes kidnaping in Illinois and other states.

"As a non-custodial parent, what is my legal obligation if my children should get into trouble while in the care of their custodial parent?"

Illinois has a parental responsibility law that makes parents liable to pay damages for the willful wrongs of their children that injure a person or property. The law does not distinguish between custodial/non-custodial parents. In addition, if there is a juvenile court action involving a child, both parents are notified even if they are divorced.

Divorce would not appear to absolve non-custodial parents from the responsibility for the crimes or misdeeds of their children. A non-custodial parent could very well obtain custody if the children are engaging in criminal behavior repeatedly due to the "neglect" of the custodial parent.

"Can a child's visitation to a homosexual parent of the same sex be terminated because of the sexual orientation of the parent?"

Legal requirements to terminate visitation are stringent. There must be an affirmative showing of actual physical or mental harm to the child, or a reasonable certainty that it will occur. Is the homosexuality of a parent harmful per se? Generally, it is doubtful that visitation rights would be terminated for this reason. Children's awareness of sexual promiscuity could be grounds to at least severely restrict visitation whether the parent is homosexual or heterosexual.

Again, the court would ask itself whether denying visitation with the homosexual parent serves the best interests of the child.

"What steps can be taken if you discover someone in the other household has taken indecent liberties with your child?"
Report it to the police. Follow their instructions.

"In the event of the death of the custodial parent, do the children automatically become the custody of the other biological parent?"
Yes. Others may sue, however, to obtain custody.

"What if children have been born into the new marriage who are attached to their half-siblings?"
One would hope there would be visitation. Stepparents have absolutely no legal rights with respect to their stepchildren. If a stepparent wants custody of a child as opposed to a biological parent, he would have to prove the unfitness of the biological parent to have custody—and would probably be contesting grandparents, aunts and uncles as well.

Grandparents in Both Households

The parents of divorced and remarried couples will find themselves having to make adjustments as well. They may lose the close contact they once had with their grand-children prior to the divorce or they may acquire step-grandchildren with their children's remarriage or both.

The fear of not being able to see grandchildren after the divorce of a son or daughter is common. One reason for this fear is the possible remarriage and relocation out of town or state by the custodial parent and, hence, the grand-children. As one grandmother stated, "Our daughter-in-law can remarry, go wherever she wants, and we may never see our grandson again."

Hard feelings from divorces are also good reason for a grandparent's fear of losing contact with grandchildren. An angry custodial parent may not only strike out at the ex-mate, but at the ex-mate's extended family as well. In these situations, unless visitation with grandparents is written in the divorce decree, there is no guaranteed visitation.

Some grandparents feel they must allow themselves to be manipulated by their ex-daughter- or son-in-law in order to ensure visitation. Sometimes the manipulation is minimal (agreeing to babysit on short notice) and sometimes it is more extreme.

One manipulative young woman asked her former in-laws for a five thousand dollar loan. Her underlying com-munication was, "If you don't care enough about your grandchildren to lend me five thousand dollars, then you must not love them enough to want to see them." The grandparents called what they thought was her bluff and refused to lend her the money. They didn't see their grand-children for three years.

Luella Davison, 1983's National Grandparent of the Year and founder of Grandparents Anonymous[1] reports that her

---

[1] Grandparents Anonymous, Sylvan Lake, Michigan, 48053, Luella Davison, Founder..

organization is working to pass legislation that will secure visitation rights for grandparents.

According to Mrs. Davison, one concern expressed by grandparents is the fear of retaliation by the other household whenever they express an opinion concerning their grandchildren's welfare. They fear their comments will be viewed as meddling and the visitation they do have will be restricted. Worse yet, they fear retaliation in the form of stricter rules or harsher punishment for their grandchildren.

Mrs. Davison felt that a major goal for grandparents should be to keep communication open between themselves, their child, their ex-daughter- or son-in-law and their grandchildren. She added, "Sometimes to keep communication open, you have to keep your mouth shut."

Grandparents need time to adjust to being a blended family just like everyone else. Although no one expects instant love toward stepgrandchildren, the grandparents can be expected to be fair. You can encourage the equal purchase of gifts and equal time spent with biological grandchildren and stepgrandchildren.

Grandparents play a very special role in your children's lives. Frequently it is the grandparents who pass family history and traditions on to their grandchildren. Although grandparents need to accept the tradition changes in your blended family, they should be encouraged to continue those traditions that are an important part of your family heritage, or the heritage of the other household.

If you are a custodial parent, arrange special times for your children to visit their grandparents from the other household. Allow some flexibility in your visitation schedule for your children to visit their other household when out-of-town grandparents come for a visit.

If you are a non-custodial parent, be considerate of your

parents' desire to see your children by including them in some of your blended family activities while your children are staying with you.

We found a list of do's and don't's for grandparents in an article by Vivian N. Doering, which gives valuable guidelines:

> Do participate in divorce proceedings to obtain visitation rights with grandchildren.
>
> Do observe faithfully the times allowed for visitation.
>
> Do continue family traditions as much as possible.
>
> Do volunteer, if parents agree, to keep the child for an extended visit during vacation time to further relationships.
>
> Do keep open the lines of communication at all times.
>
> Do be aware of the confusion the child is feeling when his natural parents break the family unit he has always known.
>
> Do be aware of any signs of emotional, mental or sexual abuse involving the child.
>
> Do respect any rules the new parents may establish.
>
> Do consider being foster grandparents to children who have no grandparents.
>
> Don't speak negatively about the new stepparent.
>
> Don't bring up taboo subjects with the child.
>
> Don't try to buy love with lavish gifts.
>
> Don't violate conditions of visitation rights.
>
> Don't violate the confidence of the child.[2]

[2] Doering, Vivian N., "Grandparents: An Endangered Species?", *Today's Woman, Decatur Herald and Review* (September 11, 1983), pp. 8-9.

Developing a Workable Relationship with the Other Household

An effective relationship between households depends in part on how you view your children's other biological parent; you are in bondage to a person you cannot forgive. Don't let unforgiveness adversely affect your relationship with the other household or the relationships in your own household. Be forgiving. Get out of bondage.

Denny is working toward a better relationship with his other household. "The kids' mother and I are not yet to the place where we can talk freely concerning the children. However, we are definitely not where we used to be. When she used to call me just to tell me what a jerk I was, I would defend myself and we would end up in one of those receiver-slamming arguments. Now when she starts in on one of those conversations, I just let her talk. I don't respond. I don't argue. I don't defend myself. I know I'm not a jerk. I don't have to feel guilty the rest of my life because things didn't work out between us, and I don't have to go around despising her. It takes two to play the game we were playing, and I'm just not going to play anymore."

If there is an ongoing battle between your households, I suggest you seek professional counseling with a therapist who has not worked with either family. If you know that many of the difficulties you are experiencing come from your inability to separate yourself emotionally or psychologically from the other household, you may want to go for individual counseling. An objective person can help you process and resolve unfinished business.

Relationships among households, grandparents and the extended family ultimately should center around everyone's desire to provide a quality life for all the children in both households.

9

A Richer Blend: Family Bonding

The clashing of individual tastes is inevitable when two family systems are attempting to merge into one. Yet when family members earnestly begin mixing their differences, they usually find that the combination makes their lives a little richer.

Mixing this richer blend may be accidental or intentional, effortless fun or hard work; it may center around joyous occasions or times of sorrow; it may happen during exciting adventures or through the nitty-gritty of daily living.

Working through differences at family meetings, getting to know one another in family activities and family work projects, communicating around the dinner table in an atmosphere of acceptance, and establishing a sense of continuity through family traditions are some of the ways your stepfamily can move toward family bonding.

Family Meetings

Family meetings, as mentioned briefly in Chapter 3, provide the place, the time and the individuals necessary to

take care of family matters—from chore distribution to rec-
ognition of individual accomplishments. There are several
important things to consider before setting up your family
meetings.

*If mates are having personal difficulties with each other they
need to settle their differences before the family meeting.* It is
inappropriate to take jabs at your mate or sabotage his or
her influence during a family meeting because you are
upset about some unrelated matter.

*It is very important for the natural parent to stay out of the way
and let the stepparent and stepchild work out their differences.*
Learning how to work through interpersonal conflicts takes
time and practice. In reference to this, one mother commented, "I was the interpreter for our family. I tried to
interpret what my children and my husband were saying to
each other in order to keep peace. I would always jump into
their conversations and say things like, 'What Sally really
means is . . . ' or 'What Stepdad really means is. . . . '
Sometimes they would all look at me and say, 'That is not
what we meant at all.'"

*Family meetings should be held on a regular basis, preferably
weekly, and at a regularly scheduled time.* There are two reasons
for this: One, if family meetings are only called when there
are problems, they become negative occasions. Two,
blended families even more than nuclear families attempt
to ignore problems or deny ill feelings. If those problems or
ill feelings are not brought out into the open, they fester and
spill out into cutting remarks, lack of cooperation, misbehavior or explosive outbursts.

*The attitude of parents toward people will greatly influence the
emotional climate of the meeting.* Do you see people as the
enemy? As naturally lazy, irresponsible and in need of
being coerced into action? Or are people allies whom you
trust, find motivated, responsible and simply in need of

assistance in planning their activities? This important difference in attitude makes or breaks a family meeting.

Meeting Time and Attendance

To make family meetings run more smoothly, select a meeting time when everyone can be present, from the youngest family member to the oldest. Plan on meeting weekly from thirty minutes to an hour. Let family members know everyone is expected to attend, but don't wait until everyone can come to start your family meetings.

Regular attendance should be expected from the children living in your household. Non-custodial children should by all means attend family meetings while in your household and be allowed to give input on family rules, regulations, vacations and other matters that directly affect them.

Getting younger children to attend a family meeting is easier than persuading adolescents. Although adolescents no longer get excited over an after-meeting treat of cookies or ice cream, they do get "excited" over plans made at meetings without them. Your adolescent will realize the importance of rearranging his activities to be at the next meeting when he discovers family plans, and rules he is expected to follow will be made whether he is present or not. If your adolescent quips, "That's not fair," or, "You can't expect me to follow that ridiculous rule," simply answer, "If you would like to discuss it or suggest a change, come to the next family meeting."

Family meetings should cover a variety of topics, including:

> Division of chores, chore deadlines and consequences if chores are not completed

Weekend and vacation plans, or other family
   activities
Establishing new rules in the household (or
   possibly abolishing old rules)
Working through concerns and complaints (e.g.,
   issues of unfairness)
Financial concerns

Family Meeting Format

Here is a suggested format for your family meetings.

Begin with prayer.
Have a devotional reading. Pass this responsibility
among family members. Depending on the age of your
children, they may read a Scripture, share something they
heard recently in Sunday school, or select a passage from a
family devotional you have available.
Discuss unfinished items from the last family meeting.
To help you remember what needs to be discussed, have
someone take notes at each family meeting. This job can be
traded or the group can select one family member.
Evaluate decisions made from the previous meeting.
Discuss complaints and concerns.
Discuss new business. For example: upcoming family
plans, scheduling the family car, menu suggestions, the
need for new purchases.
Note accomplishments, appreciations and encourage-
ments. If you want your children to be willing to attend the
next meeting, end the current one on a positive note. For
example, show appreciation for things they have done,
point out accomplishments or good behaviors you have
noted during the week, say "thank you" or "I apologize"
when appropriate and so on.

Depending on the ages of your children you may consider going out for ice cream, having dessert, sending out for pizza or ending your meeting with a family activity.

Keeping Order

To keep order during your meetings we suggest that the whole family understand and follow these four simple rules.

No one raises his voice above a normal speaking tone. Yelling and screaming beget yelling and screaming. Again, as parents you need to set the standard.

No one leaves until the family meeting is adjourned. This means no one leaves in a fit of anger or to talk on the telephone or to deal with anything that should have been dealt with before the meeting (like homework).

No one criticizes anyone else. You can ask questions but you cannot blame others.

Everyone's opinion is accepted as valid.

Problem-Solving

There may be some decisions your family will face that require a formalized problem-solving technique. We have found the following six-step technique, formulated by John Dewey, to work well for us.

Step One: Define the problem. It is important to work on one problem at a time, pinpointing exactly what the problem is and sticking to that subject. Do not discuss several things at once, go off on tangents, or introduce several other problems before solving the first one. For example, Dad may introduce a problem by saying, "Last month's power bill was too high. As a result, we are going to have to spend some of the money we had set aside for our vacation. We have to work out some way as a family to cut back on our use of power."

Step Two: Brainstorm for the solution. This is the point at which all suggestions are accepted. It is important to create an atmosphere in which everyone feels free to share his ideas. Steer clear of negative responses. "It won't work." "How could you come up with such a stupid idea?" "We already tried it." Both negative *and* positive statements ("I like that idea") should be forbidden because they pass judgment, influence other members of the family and stop the creative flow.

For each brainstorming idea introduced, acknowledge that it has been heard and will be considered later on in the process. When Jeffrey offers, "I guess I could take shorter showers," Dad should acknowledge his comment by a simple "O.K." and write it down. When Holly adds, "We could turn down the volume on the TV and save money," Dad should say unflinchingly, "O.K., Holly," and write down her suggestion.

Step Three: Evaluate the brainstorming. In this stage you discuss each of the ideas that were brainstormed and pick out the best ones. Those not feasible are removed from the list in a positive way, along with the reasons why. "Holly, your suggestion was very interesting. We appreciate your willingness to turn the TV down, but the volume doesn't affect the amount of power the TV uses."

Step Four: Decide on the most acceptable solution. Try to select a solution or solutions everyone in the family will find acceptable. Leaving the air conditioner off during the day may be very acceptable to everyone but Mom, for example, since she is the only one home during the day.

For some problems there may be several solutions, while others may require one final solution. Take the time to sit there and hammer out the answer, but remember, parents, you are the ones responsible for the welfare of your family. Ultimately, the decision is up to you.

Step Five: Develop a plan to implement the solution. Be specific. Describe what has to be done to accomplish the desired results. To save money on the power bill: The last person to leave a room will turn off the lights. Jeffrey will cut his shower time down. Mom will use cold water to do the laundry. Holly will make sure the TV is turned off when she is not watching it. And so on.

Step Six: Evaluate the success of the plan that was implemented. If the chosen solution is not working, bring it up as a new problem at the next family meeting. Just because you made a plan last week does not mean it was cast in concrete. Be flexible. It is all right to reevaluate and make changes for the better.

During family meetings you will want to keep some specific things in mind:

> Let your children know you are going to respect their opinions. This is something they will have to feel and not just be told.
> Try to pick out the important points of each child's suggestion and repeat it for the rest of the family.
> Write down all of the suggestions given during the brainstorming. We recommend buying an easel, a large pad of newsprint and a large felt-tip marker for writing down the suggestions for everyone to read.

Family meetings can play a significant role in blended family bonding. They can offer an accepting atmosphere in which each person can share ideas and learn to listen without passing judgment. They give stepsiblings the opportunity to feel assured of equal footing in the family. They also help families work on problems, solutions and goals together.

Sticking Together Through Family Activities and Outings

We were jammed into a booth at a local restaurant when the sight of a plate piled high with potato chips triggered Nichole's memory of our first family picnic.

"Hey Dad, remember our first picnic?"

"Do I remember our first picnic!"

Soon we were all laughing about the unforgettable picnic when we ate beans out of a can using potato chips as forks because Adrienne had forgotten to bring a pan and silverware and matches.

It was, in fact, a total fiasco—but not a total disaster. When I discovered that Adrienne had also forgotten the can opener, I began methodically opening the beans by pounding a screwdriver around the lid with a rock—centimeter by centimeter.

That task completed, Jennifer and I searched the car for matches. (Adrienne was used to plugging in the electric charcoal starter.)

Nichole made a gallant Girl Scout attempt at rubbing two sticks together over a clump of dried leaves to make a fire. When Jennifer and I returned from the car, without matches, Nichole retired the sticks and began striking two rocks together, regardless of the fact that neither rock was flint.

We eventually found some matches, substituted the potato chips for silverware and ate the beans right out of the crudely opened can.

If I had been impatient, if Adrienne had moaned about not being able to do anything right, if Nichole and Jennifer had been bored and whining, there is no doubt that outing would have been horrible. As it was, however, we all enjoyed a funny time that has become a favorite family joke.

Family activities are not always fun and games and may fall short of the happy closeness we have envisioned beforehand. You may find it difficult while playing a "fun game" not to lose your temper, not to think your stepchildren are selfish or your biological children are being picked on or your mate is being unfair. When planning outings with your blended family, realize there are going to be problems, hassles and disagreements. Just relax and work through them. If the biological parent knows the stepparent is going to relax during the outing, he will also be able to relax and not be hypercritical of the children's behavior.

Spontaneous Family Activities

A spontaneous family activity is one that involves the whole family on the spur of the moment. Some of these activities are more spontaneous than others. After Lou pulls out the Monopoly set and asks, "Anyone want to play?" the family may spend the whole evening around the game board. Or Stepdad may notice everyone at home is looking bored and offer, "Hey, let's go bowling, or how about swimming? Let's all go to family swim at the Y!" With that, everyone grabs swimsuits, piles into the car and heads for the pool.

One of our regular spontaneous family activities is breaking into song while riding in the car to Grandma's, church or the store. We all have our favorite songs. Adrienne and I enjoy the quiet worship songs. Jennifer likes rounds and Nichole enjoys singing songs in which she can test different harmonies. Luke's favorite is "My God is so BIG!" He especially loves it when we all yell big so loud the car vibrates.

Some of the more enjoyable times we have had as a family were ones the girls initiated. When Nichole was younger, she and Jennifer put on plays for us at least once a month. They spent hours in their room working on costumes and scripts. When they were ready to perform, one of them would deliver a flyer announcing that the play would take place in fifteen minutes. They also enjoyed performing plays in their other household with their stepsister, and in both households always found a receptive audience.

The possibility of family bonding taking place from the spontaneous activities your children and stepchildren initiate depends a great deal on how you relate to the activity. The family can respond warmly and naturally, making the activities an important part of family bonding.

Planned Family Activities

Although spontaneous activities are valuable, most families need to plan a good portion of their activities. Here are some points to consider.

What are the family members interested in? Have everyone write down favorite activities at the family meeting. They do not all have to be interested in the same activity. Judy can do what Bob likes to do one day, and Bob can do what Judy likes another.

What are activities appropriate for the children's ages?

What activities can every child participate in?

What are your family's limitations? Finances? Physical limitations?

Here is a list of twenty family activities to get you started.

Get everyone up early one morning to go walking, jogging or bike riding. Then go out for breakfast or have the family cook a big breakfast at home.

Go on a picnic or cookout. (Be sure to bring the matches, can opener and silverware.) You can all join in food preparation, games of badminton or volleyball, or sand city building in the playground sandbox.

Have a picnic in your backyard and roast hot dogs and marshmallows.

Go for a swim.

Spend the day at the lake.

Go to a baseball or football game. Every fall I take my family to a football game at my old high school.

Go fishing. Adrienne looks back with fond memories at the times her family went fishing with her dad. Her mom would sit on their old picnic blanket, braiding wool strips into a rug. Her father and older brother would cast and reel with their fishing poles down by the river bank, while she and her younger brother explored rocks and weeds and inspected the squirmy fish bait.

Go boating or waterskiing.

Spend time in the park swinging or riding the merry-go-round.

Go roller-skating or bowling.

When it snows, go for a walk, make a snow fort or build a snow family just like yours. Serve hot chocolate with marshmallows when you return.

Work on a thousand-piece jigsaw puzzle.

Go on a Coke and french fry outing.

Read a book together as a family.

Cook pretzels, doughnuts, sugar cookies or pizza together.

Have an art night. Paint or watercolor, make Christmas

cards or Valentines or experiment with modeling clay. There are several books on art projects for family fun. See, for example, *Sticks and Stones and Ice Cream Cones* by Phyllis Fiartta, *Sunset Crafts for Children* by Sunset, *Family Fun: Things to Make, Do, and Play* by Susan Stranks and *Creative Clay Design* and *Creative Paper Design* by Ernst Rottger.

Combine a family and work project, such as planting a garden, canning, cleaning the garage, washing the car, scrubbing the porch, having a rummage sale or helping Grandma with odd jobs.

Meals as Family Time

The family meal is an opportune time for communication about the day's events, the concerns of each individual and moral and spiritual issues.

There are many families whose only family time during the week is at the dinner table. Whether you are one of these families or not, make the most of the meals you have together, be it breakfast, lunch or dinner.

In Chapter 3 we approached family meals in terms of removing hostility and fostering acceptance at the table. Even during the process of displacing hostility with acceptance, some specific mealtime guidelines are appropriate. We suggest the following:

Try to plan meals in advance, with everything on the table at mealtime. The cook needs family time, too.

Wait until everyone is seated before praying and filling plates.

Eat without the television on or music blaring.

Do not accept telephone calls during mealtime. When someone calls at the dinner hour inform them you are eating and will be glad to return the call when you are finished.

Avoid "eat-and-runs" if at all possible.

Do not bring up behavioral or discipline problems at the table. If table manners are a problem, try the "napkin count" we explained in Chapter 3.

Do not allow negative comments concerning other family members. (This rule can easily be enforced by the "napkin count.")

To add fun and variety to your family meals, plan:

A classical dinner with the whole family "dressing for dinner," candlelight, classical music in the background and the good china.

A progressive dinner with soup and salad in the kitchen, the main course in the family room and dessert in one of the children's bedrooms.

A menu with dishes from other countries. For Mexican night serve tacos, burritos, sanchos, tamales, enchiladas, tostadas, cheese and nachos and taco salad. For Italian night serve spaghetti, lasagna, stuffed manicotti, tossed salad with Italian dressing and different kinds of French bread.

A baked potato bar with large baked potatoes and various toppings to choose from including: sauteed mushrooms, sauteed onions, cheese, bacon, chili, broccoli in cheese sauce, sour cream, sausage. Serve cheesecake with strawberries for dessert.

A meal that the children organize, cook and serve. Nichole and Jennifer have cooked and served several meals for us. On those evenings, Adrienne and I wait in the living room until Jennifer announces that our table is ready. She escorts us to our seats, hands us our menus and returns to the kitchen. In a few moments she is back at our table wearing an apron, and with pencil and paper in hand suggests we might like to try the special. We agree, and in no time they have served our meal, taken off their aprons and joined us at "the restaurant."

After dessert, the girls jump up, leave the room and return with their aprons on. Jennifer hands us a fake bill, we pay with fake money and leave a real tip.

Our family often has small Scripture cards waiting for us on our dinner plates at mealtime. After the blessing, we take turns reading our Scripture cards and commenting on what we think they mean. On other days when Nichole and Jennifer are feeling especially creative, we find placecards by our dinner plates with special messages written inside.

Family Traditions and Holidays

Special meals on different holidays, certain activities at different times of the year, or family celebrations of birthdays, weddings or anniversaries can all become traditions.

Traditions carry good memories from the past into the present. Family activities centered around traditions or keepsakes (a special Christmas creche or holiday recipe) that are passed from generation to generation give family members a sense of being rooted and grounded.

When a new family is created through remarriage, new traditions are established, old ones incorporated and some are shared with the other household.

The new traditions established in a blended family are either a blend of traditions both mates have brought into the marriage or something completely new. Because of Adrienne's and my family backgrounds, the blend of most of our traditions came naturally. Both of our extended families celebrate birthdays with a party, ice cream and cake. Our Christmas traditions were equally compatible. We open the presents on Christmas morning, have a special

Christmas breakfast and take plenty of "cheesy" photographs.

A blended family's new traditions are often formed out of necessity or as a direct result of trying to keep all the children entertained. In one blended family what started as an offer to help feed "the hungry crew" (his three and her two) turned into a Saturday morning pancake breakfast tradition.

Another blended family started a family tradition on the first New Year's Eve all five of their children were together. "Whenever we were together," the mother told me, "there were enough of us to stay home and have our own New Year's Eve party. So we had fireworks and sparklers and when it was close to midnight the kids would put on their coats, stand out on the front porch and wait for our signal. As soon as the clock struck twelve my husband and I would yell, 'Happy New Year!' and they would take off down the steps and run all the way around the block banging pans and shouting 'Happy New Year!' I don't know how much the neighbors enjoyed our celebration, but our children looked forward to bringing in the new year together."

Traditions shared with the other household include birthdays and holidays. Many blended family children celebrate the same occasions several times and sometimes in much the same ways. Nichole and Jennifer, for example, celebrate Christmas with their other household on Christmas Eve, with us on Christmas Day, and with the extended families from both households on various days throughout the Christmas holidays. With the right attitude in both households, holidays spent in this manner can be enjoyable for every member.

Difficulties arise when one or the other or both households are unwilling to allow their children to be rooted and grounded in the other household with family traditions.

Refusing to let children bring home Christmas presents, gifts or leftover birthday cake from their other household, or refusing visitation until the holiday or birthday is long gone, is not fair to the children or the other household. If the gifts are inappropriate for your child's age or developmental level, store them until they can use them, or talk over an appropriate replacement with the other household.

Remember that children who have experienced the breakup of a nuclear family are trying to regain their identities in two households. This means that they need to become a part of family traditions in their other household as well. Be willing to give them the freedom they need.

In I Corinthians, Paul refers to the Church as being one body with many parts. A family, blended or nuclear, is also one unit with many parts. In the following passage new words have been interchanged to fit the blended family. As you read through it, think of the bonding process at work in your household.

> Now the [family] is not made up of one [member] but of many. If the [stepchild] should say, "Because I am not a [biological child], I do not belong to the [family]," [he] would not for that reason cease to be part of the [family]. And if the [non-custodial child] should say, "Because I am not a [custodial child], I do not belong to the [family]," [he] would not for that reason cease to be part of the [family].
>
> If one [member] suffers, every [member] suffers with [him]; If one [member] is honored, every [member] rejoices with [him].
>
> (I Corinthians 12:14-16, 26)

10

Let Grace Abound

The inherent problems in a blended family system, combined with our own human weaknesses and mistakes, may at times seem like an overwhelming load. But take heart. There is also joy that can emerge like the beauty of a carefully polished gem. You can have the satisfaction of knowing you are making your best effort to develop close relationships, even though it may seem at times like a long road.

At one point Adrienne and I were going through a particularly difficult time of feeling worn out and pressured on all sides. One afternoon while driving home from an out-of-town visit, we were mulling over how we were going to meet all of our responsibilities and live the lives we thought we should. As our conversation drifted to silent contemplation, a huge semi tractor-trailer truck went zipping past us on the highway with the word *Grace* printed across its side in six-foot high letters. Whether you call it happenstance or a miracle, which we call it, Adrienne and I knew simultaneously that we were going to make it—by God's wonderful grace.

God's unmerited assistance is not limited to person or situation. Rely on God to pull you through. This is the first aspect of letting grace abound: Rely on the heavenly Father to love you enough to guide you through difficulties.

The second is closely related: As you experience God's pardon of your mistakes, pardon the mistakes of others in your blended family.

In spite of my professional training, there have been those occasions when I have failed and Adrienne and the girls have pardoned me. Likewise, there have been instances when they have failed me and I have pardoned them.

One particular time in Nichole's early teen years, she and I needed to pardon one another. I had felt hurt and rejected on several occasions by what seemed to be her pointed remarks. When I found myself wanting to respond to her with comments of my own, I knew we needed to sit down together and talk about it.

One afternoon after Nichole got home from school, I called her from the office and asked her to have dinner with me that night. She responded hesitantly, "Oh, I don't know. I have a lot of homework." With a little persistence on my part, she agreed.

After hanging up the phone, I learned later, she turned to Adrienne and asked, "Mom, do I really have to go?"

Adrienne answered, "Yes, you do," and added, "I would think you'd be delighted that your dad invited you out to eat with him."

As Nichole left the room, sulking, she called back, "You mean my *stepdad*."

I came home, picked her up, and after a few pleasantries at the dinner table got down to business.

"Where am I going wrong, Nichole? I must have done something to hurt your feelings and make you angry."

Nichole fidgeted, stared at her food and then answered, "I don't think you've done anything to hurt my feelings."

"Then why have you been acting the way you have? Why have you been treating me with such disdain?"

Her response was blunt. "I guess it's just because you're a stepdad."

Then I understood that Nichole wanted either her real dad to be at home, or else for me to be her real dad. At that difficult time of early adolescence she wanted to be able to tell her friends, "This is my dad," instead of, "This is my stepdad. My real dad lives aross town."

We were able to talk openly about the unchanging fact that I can be only Nichole's stepdad. Somehow or other she had to pardon me for playing that role in her life. At the same time, I had to pardon her for treating me like a stereotypic stepfather, instead of relating to me for who I am. In blended families, then, both parents and children will need at times to forgive one another.

The third aspect of grace is also related to recognizing God's love for you: Be merciful. This means showing compassion or forbearance to someone who has offended you. Mercy should pervade the atmosphere of your home. Love. Encourage. If you are offended, respond with the same compassion you want others to show you.

One of the interesting things about our grace truck experience is that the truck was in motion. We did not pass it parked or broken down along the highway somewhere. God's grace is like that. It never stops or breaks down, and there is always plenty to go around.

Tom and Adrienne Frydenger are available to conduct "Blended Family" seminars for your church or organization:

> Tom and Adrienne Frydenger
> Suite 106
> 151 E. Decatur
> Decatur, IL 62521

Telephone: (217) 428-0503